HNF 545

Today's World

The Japanese

Richard Tames

BATSFORD ACADEMIC AND EDUCATIONAL
LONDON

CONTENTS

© Richard Tames 1982
First published 1982
Reprinted 1985

Typeset by Tek-Art Ltd, Kent
and printed in Great Britain by
R.J. Acford
Chichester, Sussex
for the publishers
Batsford Academic and Educational
an imprint of B.T. Batsford Ltd
4 Fitzhardinge Street
London W1H 0AH

ISBN 0 7134 4453 3

THE JAPANESE

You should not think that these people are barbarians because, apart from the Faith, however prudent we may believe we are, we are great barbarians compared with them. In all truth I confess that I learn from them every day and I think that there is no other nation in the world with such and so many talents and natural gifts as the Japanese.

(Organtino Gnecchi-Soldo, 1577)

The first description of Japan to be printed in English appeared during the reign of Queen Elizabeth I. Four centuries later, in the reign of a second Elizabeth, the words still have a contemporary relevance:

Japonia may be said to be, as it were, a body of many and sundry islands, of all sorts of bigness; which isles, as they are separated in situation from the rest of the whole world, so are they, in like manner, inhabited of people, most different from all others, both for manners and customs.

The author of this passage also observed that among the most noticeable characteristics of the Japanese was the fact that

they are very punctual in the entertaining of strangers, of whom they will curiously inquire even trifles of foreign people, as of their manners and such like things.

In recent years the foreigners have begun to return the compliment. In 1970 the "futurologist", Herman Kahn's dramatically entitled book, *The Emerging Japanese Superstate*, was published. It devoted much space to analysing the causes and likely impact on the world of Japan's so-called "economic miracle". This emphasis well reflected what most Westerners were concerned about, and

many other similar books which appeared in the following decade took a similar line.

Foreigners writing about Japan have often been so charmed by its unique qualities that they have simply failed to take it seriously. Even such an experienced traveller as Rudyard Kipling could write as late as 1900, when Japan's industrialization was well advanced:

It would pay us to establish an international suzerainty over Japan: to take away any fear of invasion and annexation, and pay the country as much as ever it chose, on condition that it simply sat still and went on making beautiful things . . . . It would pay us to put the whole empire in a glass case . . . . The Japanese should have no concern with business. The Japanese has no business savvy . . .

A Japanese view of the Japanese (from a woodblock print by Hiroshige, 1858).

Spectacular monorails above the rooftops of Tokyo symbolize both Japan's advanced technology and its lack of living-space.

Perhaps recently the tide has begun to flow in the opposite direction. A tone of breathless amazement and a vague sense of being threatened sometimes permeates contemporary writing about Japan, as in the special edition on Japan produced by the French magazine *L'Histoire* in 1981:

Japan? A very distant country which intrigues us and makes us a bit uneasy . . . . A country which we know through its cinema, its platoons of identical tourists, but above all by its radios, cameras, motor-bikes and cars. . . . There isn't a meeting of the EEC without someone talking about "the Japanese danger" . . . . How has the defeated power of 1945 got into this position? . . . A great power which continues to rise and which nothing seems to stop, animated as it is by a systematic spirit of conquest. This Japanese miracle fascinates Westerners . . . . Above all, it is a country which is already living in the future. For Japan it is the present.

Books about Japan's economic miracle at least had the virtue of stimulating interest in Japan

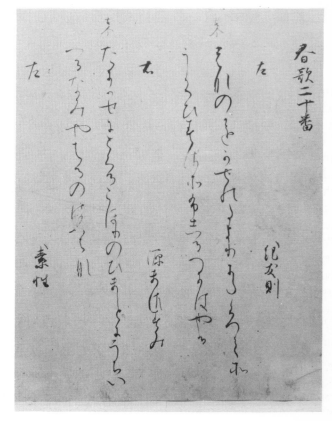

Festivals in modern Japan are less an indication of religious fervour than a testimony to the strength of traditional community feelings. *Mikoshi* — portable shrines — are usually paraded at local festivals like this.

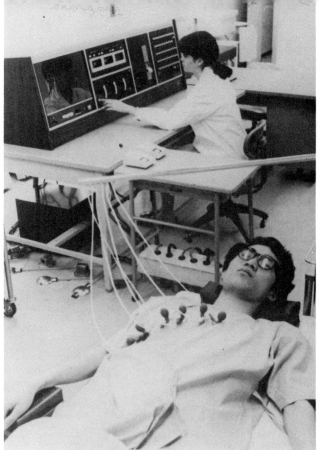

The most sophisticated medical treatment is widely available in Japan and the life-expectancy of the people is among the highest in the world.

among non-Japanese. But their perspective was often narrow and one-sided. By contrast, works written by Westerners who had lived in Japan and had made a careful study of its language, culture and institutions, called for an understanding which was not based on the pre-judgment that all that mattered about Japan was its economic success and its international implications. The very title of Frank Gibney's *Japan: The Fragile Super Power* was a challenge to Herman Kahn's characterization of the country and a reminder of how far Japan's prosperity and stability depended upon the precarious and intricate structure of world trade. Professor Ezra Vogel's *Japan as No I: Lessons for America* argued that developed nations had much to learn from Japan in such

◄ A classical Japanese poem. Poetry is widely appreciated in Japan, but few foreigners are ever able to gain sufficient mastery of the language to enable them to share this enjoyment.

fields as the control of crime, the provision of mass education and the management of the environment.

The views of writers like Gibney and Vogel seem, however, to have had relatively little impact in changing Japan's image abroad. When a Pakistani diplomat described the Japanese as "economic animals" and a senior EEC official referred to them as "a nation of workaholics living in rabbit hutches", these remarks received wide publicity in Japan and reinforced the feeling that, as a people, the Japanese are isolated and misunderstood. As the author of that sixteenth-century description of Japan noted, "they covet exceedingly honour and praise". But from foreigners they seemed rarely to receive either.

Writing in *The Japan Times* (one of four English-language dailies published in Japan) in 1981, an American businessman, Thomas E. Cappiello, argued that the West was suffering from the same problem which had plagued Imperial

▲
Tokyo cityscape. Every major city in Japan, except Kyoto, which was spared from Allied bombing, has been reconstructed since the war.

Even in crowded cities the Japanese love of nature finds expression, framing the pathway to the home.
▼

China in the nineteenth century — it had for so long been accustomed to regarding itself as the centre of world power and civilization that it simply could not take any other country seriously. As Cappiello put it,

> The Japanese challenge to Western industrial might has virtually taken the West by surprise, not because the challenge was concealed, but because it was so totally unexpected.

Very little serious news about Japan is carried by the mass media in Western countries and only a handful of the so-called "foreign correspondents" based in Tokyo can speak Japanese with any competence. (And many of them are expected to cover East and South East Asia as well — that is, half the population of the world.) Equally important in Cappiello's view is the neglect of Japan by the education systems in Europe and North America:

> Most children in the West go through 12 years of schooling having never learned more about Japan than its location and the name of its largest city. University graduates do not know who Japan's prime minister is or even that there is a significant difference between the Chinese and Japanese languages. The literally 'self-centred' orientation of Western education has undoubtedly reinforced the notion that there is little to learn from Japan . . .

But what is there to learn from Japan? According to Alvin Toffler, another American futurologist, Westerners who are aware of Japan's importance pay far too much attention to the achievements of the 1960s and ignore the promise of the 1980s. They are fascinated by Japan's proficiency in producing steel, ships and motor cars, largely because these industries are in difficulties in the West, whereas they should be interested in the growth areas of the future, particularly microelectronics. Equally, they ignore the social significance of Japanese agriculture and retail distribution, sectors which in strictly economic terms are hopelessly unproductive, but which provide valued employment and permanent "temporary"

Mechanized politeness. An electric-powered doll greets customers endlessly from a shop window.

8

refuge for those displaced by the process of industrial change. According to Toffler, the real lesson to be learned from the Japanese is that they *expect* change and know how to live with it. As an example, he mentions the *Asahi Shimbun*, the non-communist world's largest circulation newspaper, which switched over to computer printing without losing a single job or a single edition. Toffler also suggests that Westerners have as much to learn from Japan's dissidents — its well-organized opponents of environmental pollution, nuclear power and authoritarian planning — as from its production technologists and statesmen. Japan, he suggests, has become a convenient scapegoat for Western political and industrial leaders who wish to explain away their own shortcomings. What they really need to learn, Toffler argues, is *how* to cope with change

The open expression of strong emotions is rare in everyday situations, but the traditional Kabuki theatre is different. Grief, rage and shame are powerfully expressed with voice and gesture.

as the Japanese have done — without generating political instability, uncontrolled inflation or massive unemployment. It is an achievement more worthy of careful analysis than of dismissive condemnation.

One good way of starting would be to become more aware of how the Japanese see themselves. Fortunately, there is no lack of material, for a preoccupation with national identity is a prominent Japanese characteristic and leads to the continuous production of a flood of books, surveys and statistics on every aspect of Japanese society.

To a Westerner, and especially to the class-conscious English, one of the most startling aspects of the Japanese self-image is the fact that no less than 90% of the population consider themselves to be middle-class. And, in terms of life-style, the statistics produced by the country's Economic Planning Agency bears this out — 99% of all homes have a refrigerator, a washing-machine and a colour TV. According to Professor Taira Kori of the University of Illinois, Japan's well-known overcrowding has a positively democratizing influence because it hinders the development of slum ghettoes or exclusive, affluent suburbs:

The use of land in Japan is the embodiment of tolerance. Divisions of land and the selling of lots are carried out with no restrictions . . . large homes are interspersed with small, and non-residential structures. Because of this people of all types and occupations live in the same area . . .

According to Professor Taira, Japanese see more prestige in working for a famous company than in living in a fashionable area. Dick Wilson, a former editor of the *Far Eastern Economic Review*, sees the Japanese sense of classlessness as a major ingredient in the country's recipe for economic growth:

> The key to the success of Japanese management is surely the underlying egalitarianism, a sort of democratic mutual consideration which so often appears in Japanese society.

The Japanese very much wish to be understood by foreigners. In 1980 a book called *Misunderstanding* was published. It traced the history of Japanese and Western attempts to learn about each other's customs and cultures. It was written by a Japanese-speaking Englishman. It became a best-seller, where it was published — in Japan.

Cranes, symbol of long life and health, decorate a black lacquer tray, laid on tatami matting, the traditional floor-covering of a Japanese home. Simple elegance is a characteristic feature of the Japanese sense of beauty.

WORK

As to all sorts of handicrafts, either curious or useful, they are wanting neither proper materials, nor industry and application, and so far is it that they should have any occasion to send for masters from abroad, that they rather exceed all other nations in ingenuity and neatness of workmanship . . .

(Engelbert Kaempfer, ca.1694)

Writing on the eve of the 1981 Frankfurt International Motor Show, the motoring correspondent of the *Times* observed that:

What frightens European manufacturers is not so much the numbers of Japanese cars as the almost devastating efficiency with which they are made. Japan is about three times as productive as Britain and twice as productive as the most efficient European motor industry, West Germany . . . . It is hard to see, without fundamental changes in working practices and attitudes, how Europe can ever close the gap.

What is true of motor cars is also true of a wide range of modern industrial products, such as motor cycles, colour TV sets, radios, cassette players, cameras and calculators. Japan has entirely left behind its pre-war reputation for

Artificial islands crowd the coastline to enable industries to cut the transport costs of imported raw materials and manufactured goods for export.

producing cheap, shoddy junk and has now become a by-word for goods which are well-designed, well-made, reliable and very competitively priced.

It must be appreciated that, while the Japanese were largely driven by the need to reconstruct their war-shattered country in the 1950s and '60s, by the 1970s their economy was forced to adjust to the devastating impact of constantly rising oil prices. Having so little in the way of domestic energy resources, Japan became heavily dependent on imported oil which came to provide 90% of its energy needs. By 1980 the price of crude oil was more than eight times what it had been in 1973. Japanese industry coped with the situation by slimming down and improving fuel-efficiency in those sectors which were energy-intensive (for example, steel) and by boosting exports to pay for the fuel which the country had to have. By 1980 oil still accounted for 37.5% of Japan's import bill (the UK figure was 7.6%); and whereas in 1973 Japan had had to export 9.7 tons of steel or 10.7 colour TV sets to pay for 100

kilolitres of crude oil, by 1980 the figures had risen to 40.1 tons of steel or 77.1 colour TV sets for the same amount. Appraising this achievement, the *Financial Times* noted approvingly that:

> Japan's economic performance has outclassed that of every other Western industrial country in dealing with the oil shocks — real GNP growth has been the fastest among OECD members, productivity has grown more quickly and unemployment has stayed low. Inflation has always been below the OECD average . . .

There is no one "secret" to explain Japan's phenomenal post-war industrial success; and many obvious reasons, such as a massive home market (about twice the size of the home markets of Britain, France or West Germany), are often overlooked. A willingness to adopt — and adapt — the latest production technology is certainly an important factor. During the 1950s and 1960s Japanese industrialists showed themselves willing to borrow heavily and plough back a high proportion of their profits in order to invest in new plant and equipment. By the 1970s Japan was

Pickets outside a small workshop. Strikes in Japan usually take place in April, when the "spring struggle" marks the beginning of a new financial year.

Precision, quality and reliability have become watchwords for Japanese industry.

also leading the way in the introduction of industrial robots.

But machines do not run themselves. They have to be chosen, maintained and, in due course, scrapped. And it is significant that, in the paragraph quoted on page 11, the motoring correspondent of the *Times* does not mention technology as a factor in closing the productivity gap between Europe and Japan, but rather stresses the need for "fundamental changes in working practices and attitudes".

Japanese Workers

The diligence and loyalty of the Japanese worker have now become almost legendary. But it is less often appreciated that he is also very well educated and thus not only able to handle advanced technology but also capable of discussing its use and problems with managers whose education has been very similar to his own and who neither speak nor act like a separate and superior caste.

The 1981 survey of the Japanese economy by the Organization for Economic Co-operation and Development (OECD) supported the view that the Japanese worker's loyalty to his company is very rational, because the biggest single factor in deciding basic wage rates is each firm's performance rather than the cost-of-living increases or the "going rate" for the job. And bonus payments, which account for about a quarter of average take-home pay, are even more closely tied to profitability.

The *Daily Express* noted in a leading article in March 1981:

What comes out of most studies of Japanese industry is the central importance of close co-operation between management and workers. Our blinkered class war seems incomprehensible to them.

Yet Japanese firms which have set up in Britain have been successful . . . A hundred years ago they looked to us as the chief industrial nation. After the war, we helped put their car industry together. Now it is our turn to learn.

Not all Western commentators have taken this attitude.

The Japanese Explain Their Success

In the 1960s the Japanese were so flattered by the growth of Western interest in their "economic miracle" that they were largely content to let the Westerners explain it to each other as best they could. By the 1970s, as Japan's growing economic power attracted more and more criticism from disgruntled industrial rivals, the Japanese saw the need to challenge hostile analyses and charges of "conspiracy" and "unfair trading", and to offer their own account of the basis of their success. One example of this effort to explain was a pamphlet on *The Japanese-Style Economic System* (1981) written by two university professors, Yatsuhiro Nakagawa and Nobumasa Ota, and distributed free to Western journalists through Tokyo's Foreign Press Centre. In this pamphlet the authors argue that the Japanese economy is distinctively different from both the centrally-directed economies of the Soviet Union and its allies, and the market-oriented mixed economies of the capitalist world. But it is not, they suggest, simply a peculiar and unique hybrid but rather a model of an advanced industrial society from which others might learn much to their advantage. They point, in particular, to the following features as worthy of study and reflection:

1. The limited role of direct government intervention in the economy. In 1979 taxes and welfare payments accounted for 31.2% of the national income in Japan, while in Britain they represented 46.2%. In 1975 65% of research and development in Japan was paid for by private organizations; in Britain the figure was only 41%. And while a British Conservative government was giving large cash subsidies to motor manufacturers, shipyards and the computer and aerospace industries, in Japan the public sector was actually being cut back. In Japan, direct interference in business management by government is very rare, and so is detailed regulation of its

activities. But the government and the Bank of Japan are expected to step in with funds if the bankruptcy of a particular firm threatens to set off a chain-reaction among its trading partners.

2. The way money is channelled into industry in Japan. In Western countries private firms who wish to invest raise money by selling shares to individuals, pension funds and so on. In Japan, by contrast, people and firms with money to invest put it into banks, which in turn lend to industry, either directly or through great trading houses specializing in industrial investment. Investors can thus spread their risks and take advantage of the expert knowledge of the specialists, who act as the link between lenders and borrowers. The banks, in their turn, are supervised by the Bank of Japan, which, working in close co-operation with the Ministry of Finance, suggests that certain forms of investment might, from the national point of view, prove more fruitful than others. Foreign observers have called this system "Japan Incorporated" and criticized it as a form of industrial conspiracy. The Japanese emphasize that the relationships between the component parts of the system are not based on compulsion, as in a Soviet-type economy, but on constant consultation. Thus Nakagawa and Ota conclude that:

> In advanced industrial societies, individual investors lack information and other means of supervising the management of the firms they have invested in . . . companies that invest in other companies have their hands full managing their own business . . . . For both these types of investors, a very rational answer to their needs is to have organisations specialising in investments (such as banks) take care of all investment matters.

3. The system of "life-time employment". By recruiting workers and managers at the beginning of their careers and guaranteeing them employment for life, a Japanese company is able not only to build up a strong sense of commitment among its workforce but also to organize in detail the training of each member. Expensively-acquired skills are never lost to vital companies because a worker thinks he can get better wages or promotion elsewhere, and the risks and costs involved in

At this wedding, workmates of the married couple will be as numerous as their relatives.

taking on outsiders in mid-career are eliminated. Nakagawa and Ota proclaim confidently that:

> it is fundamentally mistaken to emphasize the uniqueness of Japan's traditional recruitment policies . . . . In any advanced industrial society, the longer and more diligently workers apply themselves to jobs within the same workplace, the more the commodity value of the labour increases. Hence the most rational economic mode is one that encourages workers not to change jobs . . . . The use of such an expression as "Japanese-style management" is inappropriate for it connotes something peculiar to Japan. Such practices as life-time employment should rather be regarded as a form of management that will become universal in all advanced industrial societies.

4. The method of decision-making. In Western companies the key decisions about products, prices, markets and technology are made by top management, with middle- and lower-level managers acting only as sources of information. By contrast, Japanese companies favour making decisions by consensus, with ideas and suggestions, as well as information, flowing down *and up* the management pyramid. It can be very time-consuming, but it does enable decisions to be based on the entire available pool of knowledge and experience and for their possible consequences to be looked at from every part of the organization. Morale is built up by spreading the sense of participation; and the feeling that no one below top management has any responsibility except to follow orders is correspondingly diminished. Japanese managers argue that their counterparts in other democracies suffer tensions and a sense of indignity because the generally approved values of freedom and equality are so rarely a part of their everyday experience at work.

Nakagawa and Ota conclude their analysis with a warning:

> Economists studying Japan's economy have failed to appreciate that their central concepts, such as market economy as opposed to planned economy, private versus centralized authority, are not very meaningful in Japan's case . . . . Scholars have so far been able to ignore Japan

▲
Eating noodles at a railway foodcounter. The service industries are large providers of employment.

Not everyone works in an impressive new factory. The "dual structure" of Japanese economy also depends upon thousands of small workshops producing components for the motor and electronics industries or simple consumer goods, like pencils.
▼

because its economy was small .... But Japan is no longer small enough to be safely overlooked.

Imai Kenichi, another professor of economics, draws rather different conclusions from Japan's business success. So far, he argues, Japanese corporations have shown great skill in identifying overseas markets and providing the goods consumers want. This strategy has boosted Japan's export earnings, but it has also led to friction with trading partners whose own industries have had to struggle to compete with Japan's "invasion" of their territories. Now it is time, Imai suggests, for Japanese corporations to use their problem-solving powers in other areas, such as energy development and urban renewal. These are fields in which Japan has great problems, as do Britain, the USA and West Germany. In other words, Japanese and foreign interests in such matters are in parallel rather than in conflict. Because corporations can command massive pools of technical and managerial talent, Imai emphasizes that they should not only "think big" but also "think long-term". They should use the creative powers that put the "bullet train" into service as long ago as 1964 to solve the problems of the 1990s. Hard work, he concludes, is not enough.

MAJOR JAPANESE EXPORT ITEMS

	Production ('000)	% Exported
Cameras	12,860	76
Watches	105,224	82
Motorcycles	7,063	50
Videocameras	13,134	81
Colour TVs	11,423	52
Microwave ovens	2,314	59
Electronic calculators	58,438	77

CARS

In Tokyo itself, the capital of the empire, the roads are a scandal.

(Basil Hall Chamberlain, 1904)

Japan is the largest producer and exporter of motor cars in the world. But the modern Japanese car industry is barely a quarter of a century old. A study of its growth and impact can tell us not only much about the recent development of the Japanese economy but also a great deal about how the Japanese have tackled problems relating to technology, pollution, planning and all that they imply for the quality of life in a modern industrial society.

First came the cars. Only afterwards did the provision of adequate roads begin. This highway links Tokyo and its airport.

The Growth of the Motor Industry

What factors have encouraged the growth of the post-war Japanese motor industry? War-time production of military vehicles, trucks and aircraft created a skilled labour force and developed important subsidiary industries, such as ball-bearings. The post-war growth of industries like steel, heavy engineering, chemicals and electrical goods supplied the motor industry with low-cost, good-quality basic materials and components. And from 1952 onwards it was official government policy to encourage the development of motor vehicle manufacture by means of special financing and tax concessions and strict limits on imports of foreign-made cars. Because it was often difficult for individuals to get a personal

loan from a bank at that time, the government also sponsored a new hire purchase system, to help the industry to sell to eager customers. Governments have also placed few restrictions on the siting of factories, which has been helpful for industrialists, but not so good for the environment. Finally, one must note the willingness of the Japanese to learn from foreigners. Until 1957 Nissan, one of Japan's "Big Two" car makers, simply assembled parts imported from Britain; and its first production lines were laid out with the help of expert advisers from the Austin car plant in Britain. Toyota's was based on the Packard plant in Detroit.

By the late 1950s economic recovery had opened up an expanding domestic market for private cars. Between 1961 and 1969 the number of new car owners grew by 30% each year. (In Britain over the same period the figure was 3.7%.) Until 1970 more than 70% of cars made in Japan were sold in Japan.

The expansion of the motor industry had far-reaching effects on the growth of the Japanese economy as a whole. The end-products of some of the nation's most dynamic industries were the basic raw materials and components of motor manufacture. Motor manufacturing absorbs half of all imported rubber and about two thirds of the total output of springs, aluminium castings and metal alloys.

The growth of the motor industry likewise gave an immense boost to construction (expressways and suburban housing), commerce (insurance and shipping of vehicles for export) and a wide range of service occupations, from taxi drivers to traffic policemen.

Diversification

Japanese motor manufacturers are now branching out into new products. Some use the same or similar methods of production as those used to manufacture motor vehicles. Others require different techniques of production, but appeal to the same or similar customers. By producing a wider range of products, manufacturers are able to offset the effects of a fall in demand for one particular product by switching surplus labour, factory-space and machinery to the production of other, more successful products. This "diversification" of output acts as a sort of insurance policy, in the long-term as well as in the short-term. If oil-price rises or stricter standards of pollution control or restrictions on exports make conventional motor cars uneconomical, manufacturers should be able to develop other products to make up for the loss of output.

Some recent examples of diversification by Japanese motor manufacturers include:

Toyota — pre-fabricated housing; air-conditioning equipment

Suzuki — pre-fabricated housing

Honda — farm machinery; food processing

Toyo Kogyo (Mazda) — bicycles; precision machinery

Fuji — light aircraft.

The Japanese Car Worker

The Japanese car worker enjoys a standard of living as high as his opposite number in Britain (though he will probably live in a smaller house), but his conditions of employment will differ in a number of important respects. He will work for the same company throughout his working life, joining it when he leaves school and leaving only to retire. There is no law against leaving a company, but it is very unusual. Anyone who left would probably have to take a heavy cut in wages. His new employer would, in any case, be suspicious of his reasons for leaving. In most cases, when an employee threatens to leave, his foreman and workmates and their wives will do all they can to persuade him and his wife to stay and resolve their difficulties.

As a lifelong employee, he will expect his company to give him absolute job security. If there is a recession he may lose some overtime, but will depend on his bosses to find some sort of work for him to do. If new advances in technology make his skills redundant, he will look to his company for re-training without loss of pay or seniority. He will get an automatic pay-rise every year, regardless of his performance. If his work and time-keeping have been bad, he will get less than the average rise, but he will still get something. (He will also get a lot of pressure to improve from his foreman and workmates.) On average, a man of 50 can expect to earn 2½ times as much as a man of 20, even if they are doing the same work. For special skills and good time-keeping he can obviously expect to earn even more. He will also expect a rise when he gets married, and when each of his children is born.

He will receive not only a monthly wage but a bonus of about 2 months' wages at the New Year and again at the Midsummer Bon Festival. He will also get a free work-uniform, subsidized canteen meals, assistance with travel expenses and a wide range of fringe benefits which in other countries are normally provided by the state (subsidized housing; medical and dental services; sick pay and old-age pension schemes; educational scholarships for his children).

His social life will be largely organized around the company. He will go on outings and holidays with groups of his workmates. His wife may well take flower-arranging classes run by the company. If he is a sportsman, he will play for a company team and train in a company gym.

He will belong to the company trade union and so will all his workmates, including the junior managers. (In Japan, unions are not organized on a craft basis; there are no unions of boiler-makers or metal-workers, for example.) His wage-rates will be settled by long and complicated negotiation each year at the time of the "spring offensive". There may well be a strike, but it will last only a few days at most, usually only a few hours. Because he is an employee for life, to inflict a damaging strike on his company is to destroy his own future prospects and job security.

These conditions apply to most of the people who work for large companies, but not to all of them. Some are only temporary employees who enjoy few fringe benefits and may be laid off during a recession. And the employees of the many small firms which sub-contract for the big companies, making components such as switches and wheel trims, are at a similar disadvantage in terms of rewards and security.

The Success of Japanese Car Manufacturers

When trying to explain why Japanese motor manufacturers have been so successful in exporting to Western countries, many Western writers have argued that the Japanese were able to produce cheap cars because they paid their workers low wages. This is an inadequate explanation for two reasons. In the manufacture of motor vehicles labour is not the only, or even the most important cost. The price of energy and materials can also be crucial. And since the late 1960s — before Japan became a major car exporter — Japanese motor workers have been paid as well as, if not actually better than, motor workers in Coventry or Detroit.

How, then, have the Japanese managed to be so successful? Japanese car workers produce more per man per hour. Because most Japanese factories were bombed out during the war, they have been completely re-equipped with the latest machinery, laid out in the best possible way. The same is also true of other industries which supply the motor industry, such as steel. And so manufacturers have a double bonus: higher productivity in their own industry and low costs from their suppliers.

Japanese manufacturers usually kept up a high level of investment in new machinery throughout the 1950s and 1960s. The result has been to give each worker more and better tools and machines than his rivals overseas. In 1963 the Toyota plant produced 20 cars per employee per year; in 1969 it produced just under 40 — about twice as high as the European average, four times as high as British Ford and six times as high as British Leyland.

The government has encouraged a high rate of investment by giving special tax allowances. This has meant that the government has not collected taxes that it might have done, and has therefore not had as much revenue to spend on such things as housing, hospitals and schools. In other words, as a nation, Japan has boosted its industrial capacity at the expense of opportunities for improving welfare facilities and preserving the environment.

Because Japan has such a large home market, manufacturers have been able to produce very large numbers of a limited range of models, thus achieving great savings on specialized equipment, bulk purchase of raw materials and components etc. A wider range of models would inevitably mean shorter production runs, higher prices and therefore a more limited market. Dealers can still offer the customer something special and different by varying the colour, trim and fittings on each basic model.

Japanese manufacturers have been willing to adapt their products to suit the needs of particular countries (for example, by strengthening shock absorbers and suspension for countries with bad roads; or by making deeper seats on models for export to the West, where the average driver is two or three inches taller). They have also been willing to take a long-term view, patiently establishing dealer networks and even operating at a loss for several years while building up a reputation for quality and reliability. Japanese car-makers also advertise extensively.

Because production is so rarely disrupted by strikes in Japan, dealers have been able to make firm promises about delivery dates for cars and parts — and keep them. (Between 1958 and 1974 neither Toyota nor Nissan lost a single hour of production through strikes.) And, by building their own specially-designed ships for exporting their cars, Toyota reduced damage in transit from 40% to less than 5%. This sort of service obviously appeals to customers who have been put off buying a rival car by a long waiting-list or who have been kept off the road by the dealer's failure to deliver a needed part on time. Japanese manufacturers have therefore been able to take advantage of the failings of their rivals. When British manufacturers first began to worry about Japanese competition in the early 1970s, the motoring correspondent of the *Times* noted:

> . . . we asked readers earlier this year to give their reasons for buying Japanese. There were some negative factors, notably the long waiting lists for British cars, but it did seem that people had looked at all the alternatives in their price range and decided that the Japanese car offered the best value for money. The cars are competitively priced and tend to include as standard equipment items like heated rear windows, wing mirrors and radios which normally cost extra. But underlying the choice of a Japanese car was the feeling that . . . it would be reliable. Judging from our readers' experiences this reliability is not a myth and we have had several letters telling of trouble-free motoring over . . . 20,000 miles. Certainly the factory inspections carried out in Japan seem unusually rigorous. . .

Japanese Roads

The rapid spread of motorized transport, and especially of private car ownership in Japan itself has had unintended consequences which are far from pleasant — namely, noise, congestion, accidents and pollution.

Most Japanese cities have developed without the benefit of planning. Streets tend to be narrow because land is very expensive. They are therefore ill-suited to heavy traffic. The results have been delays for travellers and unwanted noise and danger for the residents of the areas through which they pass. According to the police, traffic jams were three times worse in 1972 than they had been in 1968. The construction of parking lots, garages and fly-overs has damaged the urban environment by taking over space that otherwise might have been used for parks or playgrounds and by blocking out sunlight and fresh breezes from low-lying areas.

Since 1946 some 300,000 Japanese have been killed in traffic accidents, more than the total number of casualties inflicted by the atomic bombs dropped on Hiroshima and Nagasaki. Traffic casualty figures rose alarmingly throughout the 1950s and 1960s, but since the peak year of 1970 they have declined rapidly. By 1975 the number of road deaths had fallen to the 1959 figure, although the number of vehicles on the road had increased ten-fold over the same period. In terms of traffic accidents, Tokyo is now a safer city than Paris, New York or even London.

How has the reduction of the accident rate been achieved? The following factors have all played a part:
1. Tougher and more widespread enforcement of traffic regulations. In 1974 there were no fewer than 8.8 million arrests for violations — out of a driving population of thirty million. The ¥ 40 million collected in fines were used for road improvements, buying extra ambulances, etc.
2. Massive expenditures on extra road-markings, signs and pedestrian guard rails.
3. The installation of computerized traffic signal systems in thirty-one major cities.
4. The introduction of special lanes for buses and bicycles.
5. Compulsory courses in safety training every time a driver renews his licence.

6. Strict inspection of vehicles to check for defective parts.

7. Repeated safety campaigns for small children organized by women's groups.

Tokyo's traffic problems during the 1950s and 1960s show very clearly the price that was paid for putting economic growth ahead of other considerations. The improvements which have taken place since then show how effective intelligent traffic-management can be.

Accidents were by no means the only hazard resulting from Tokyo's road system. In 1959 the Fire Defence Agency staged an emergency exercise in which fire engines were sent from every part of the city to an imaginary fire in the Ginza, Tokyo's main shopping area. The first to arrive took one minute and forty seconds — to travel 360 metres! Ten years earlier it had been timed at 18 seconds. Failure to bring any major fire rapidly under control would have the most appalling consequences in Tokyo, a massive sprawling city with many narrow streets and very few open spaces capable of serving as fire-breaks.

Another worsening problem was traffic congestion. A monster jam occurred on 20 September 1960, when a truck broke down outside a department store, a traffic accident happened a few streets away and a steady drizzle made driving conditions that much worse. For five hours, an area of 6 square kilometres was thrown into utter chaos as traffic was reduced to an average speed of 2½ kph. A traffic expert made the gloomy prediction that:

the government authorities are unlikely to take any steps to ease the traffic congestion until something drastic happens such as the Prime Minister being unable to get to a Cabinet meeting on time or a national guest being forced to wait at Haneda Airport because his official car is unable to arrive on time.

During the 1960s, however, a number of steps were taken to improve traffic conditions, including:
— heavier fines for traffic violations.
— installation of better street-lighting and more traffic signals.
— better marking of roads and crossings.
— better driver-training programmes and more safety education in schools.
— construction of 1,000 pedestrian footbridges over busy streets and intersections.

By 1976 road congestion had been eased and the number of traffic deaths cut to 382 (from 1,126 in 1959), despite a five-fold increase in traffic over the same period. The cost of improving the city's traffic system has been largely offset by the very large savings on fuel, made possible by the smoother flow of traffic.

Parking in cities is a major headache for the motorist.

FAMILY

In pre-war Japan, when the economy was dominated by farmers and craftsmen, the family was usually an economic as well as a social unit. Children learned how to read and write from their teachers at school, but it was at home and from their parents that they learned about work and house-keeping. As head of the household, the father had absolute authority. As organizer of the household, the mother led a life which was an endless cycle of cooking, sewing and cleaning. Forty years of continuous change have transformed this pattern dramatically.

War took millions of men from their homes and forced women to take over not only their responsibilities in the family, but, in many cases, their jobs as well. This trend to equalizing the position of men and women was strengthened by

the reforms of the American Occupation period (1945-51), which gave all citizens equal rights in law, regardless of sex, and abolished the custom of giving the largest share of the family inheritance to the eldest son.

Rapid economic growth then produced a variety of unforeseen changes. By attracting people to the cities, it disrupted village communities and obliged families to accept more cramped housing conditions. By greatly increasing the proportion of employees to self-employed persons, it made the family business the exception rather than the rule. By improving diet and medical services at the same time as it extended the normal period (and thus the expense) of education, it vastly increased the proportion of old people as it rapidly diminished the proportion of young ones — and so the relationship between the generations was profoundly altered. And, because the employees of large companies are liable to be moved several

Danchi — apartment houses. Few Japanese are satisfied with their housing conditions.

times in the course of their careers, it committed millions of Japanese families to a way of life which made it impossible to sink "roots" permanently in any one community.

Given such rapid and radical changes, it is scarcely surprising that many commentators on the Japanese scene have been tempted to speak of "the crisis of the Japanese family" or even "the break-up of the Japanese family". But do the facts bear out the sensational headlines which appear in the newspapers? While illegitimate births as a proportion of total births have been rising dramatically since the mid-1960s in Scandinavian countries, the USA, Britain and West Germany, in Japan they have actually declined. And the ratio of divorces to the total number of married couples was lower in 1977 than it had been in 1950 — and less than half what it was in Britain.

This is not to say that family life in Japan is free from strain. Because fathers often have to commute long distances, work at weekends and go drinking with colleagues or clients in the evenings, they may become strangers to their own children, unable to discipline them, help them or set them an example. Mothers, released from pre-war drudgery by electrical appliances, ready-made clothes and convenience foods, may, by contrast, lavish too much attention on their children, stifling their independence, or press them too hard to achieve examination success, only to find that they turn against them and leave them isolated in old age.

The Young and the Old

Old age is coming to preoccupy the Japanese more and more. Retirement age in Japan is still nominally 55 (and actually around 57), reflecting the low life expectancy of the pre-war period. But the proportion of the population over 65 has risen from 4.9% in 1950 to 8.6% in 1978 and is projected to double again by the first decade of the next century. With a life expectancy of 72.97 years for men and 78.33 years for women, Japan is considerably in advance of Britain and has surpassed even Sweden in the longevity of its population. On the one hand, this is a splendid indication of the rapid post-war rise in dietary standards, health care and environmental conditions;

but, on the other, it implies vast future expenditure on income maintenance, medical services and specialized housing, and basic changes in the retirement age and seniority wage system.

As a result of a sustained rise in longevity, coupled with a sharp decline in the birth rate, Japan's population as a whole is aging at a faster rate than that of any other country at any time in history. It costs, on average, about 5 times as much to provide medical care for a person over 65 as it does for someone in the 15-44 age bracket. And whereas, in 1980, each Japanese pensioner was supported by contributions from almost 13 wage-earners, by the year 2000 there will be fewer than 4 workers to every pensioner. There is, moreover, the need to provide older people with a continuing sense of purpose in life. In Japan, the proportion of people over 65 who are still actually in some kind of work (although many of them are, in theory, retired) is much

Leisure — or enforced idleness?

24

Japan's younger generation emphasizes fashion, with the accent on casual styles from America or France.

higher than in Western countries — more than 25% as opposed to less than 10%. And more than 80% of those in the 50-64 age group affirm that they want to go on working as long as they can. In Japan, for many of the older generation, work is still *"ikigai"* — what one lives for. Care of the aged in every sense is likely to figure as Japan's number-one problem in the field of welfare in the coming decades.

But it is young people rather than the old who have been most constantly the subject of public discussion in post-war Japan. A rise in juvenile delinquency has concerned parents and public commentators alike. The pressures of Japan's highly competitive educational system have left scarcely a family unscathed. Newspapers and magazines have publicized the disorderly behaviour of motorcycle gangs and the outlandish dress and manners of would-be trend-setters. A 1980 survey by the Youth Bureau of the Prime Minister's Office attempted to find out what the attitudes of young people in the 15-19 age group really were. According to this survey:

1. More than 72% said they wanted an "individual life-style", as opposed to 13% who aimed at personal distinction and 9% who wanted a life useful to others. The contrast with the pre-war period, with its emphasis on achievement and service to the community, is very marked. However, responses to a questionnaire do not necessarily indicate how young people will actually think and behave when they are a few years older and in rather different circumstances.

2. It is also notable that the percentage of young people who say that they "do not care about conventions" is considerably higher than it was twenty years ago — 43% as opposed to 29%. But the overwhelming majority of 15-19 year olds, it must be remembered, submit to wearing school uniforms without protest and practically never play truant.

3. This may be because two thirds of the young people in the sample think that academic qualifications are an advantage in present-day society. It is also noteworthy that three quarters say that their parents are affectionate towards them and try to understand their point of view. Perhaps this is why only 23% of males and 15% of females

The new generation. A month-old baby is ceremonially presented to the gods at a Shinto shrine.

say that they already consider themselves to be adults.

The 1980 Youth Survey compared current attitudes with those of twenty years ago. Another survey conducted in 1977-78, of the 18-24 age group, compared the views of Japanese young people with those of the young people of ten other countries. The figures for Japan and Britain bring out some interesting contrasts. In Britain a far higher proportion of people aged 18-24 were married (32.4%) than in Japan (11.5%). In fact, Japan had the lowest proportion of young marrieds of all the eleven countries studied and Britain the second highest, surpassed only by India (33.7%). Of those Japanese who were married, a far higher proportion (29.3%) were living with their parents than in Britain (4.2%), and a much smaller proportion of the unmarried were sharing a home with non-family members (i.e. flat-mates) — 4.6% as opposed to 15.1%. On the other hand, more than twice as large a proportion of young Japanese as of young Britons were still in full-time education — 35.6% as opposed to 15.9%. An even more striking contrast is to be found in regard to religion. No less than 70.9% of young Japanese claimed to have "no religious belief", whereas the comparable figure for young Britons was only 13.6%.

Despite the differences between Japan and Britain in the proportion of married people and of those living alone, only a very small percentage of young people in either nation claimed to have had an unhappy home life (1.6% in Japan; 2.8% in Britain), and a large percentage (about 80%) in both nations said that they were well able to talk over their problems with their parents. Where there were real clashes between parents and children, they seemed to be over remarkably similar matters — life-style (clothes, dress, spending money), "outlook on life" and relationship with the opposite sex (in that order). It is notable, however, that a significantly higher proportion of young Britons (77.0%) than Japanese (58.2%) said that their father was "sure of himself" on matters of discipline and education, and that an ideal father would be one who put his family before his job (87.3% of young Britons as opposed to 40% of Japanese).

With regard to work, young people in both countries said that life outside their job gave them more satisfaction than work itself. But a significantly larger minority in Japan than in Britain said the reverse (30.5% as opposed to 20.7%). This is consistent with the fact that 71.5% of the Japanese sample had never changed their jobs, whereas this was true of only 41.4% of the British group. 12.2% of the British group had changed jobs four times or more, but only 1.3% of the Japanese had done so. 35.4% of young Japanese said that their major goal in life was to get rich, whereas only 11.2% of the British supported this view. They opted overwhelmingly rather "to live as I like" (63.4%). Only 41.2% of young Japanese put this at the top of their list.

Considering the different backgrounds to life of the young people questioned in the survey — the relative economic and political difficulties encountered by Britain as opposed to the success of Japan over the last decade — it is very striking that a higher proportion of the British sample (82.7%) than of the Japanese sample (59.4%) pronounced themselves to be happy and hopeful about their lives. The British were also more proud of their nationality (82.6%, as opposed to 70.4%) and, when asked to say what their country has to be proud of, were much more positive in specifying its assets:

Do you think that your country has something to be proud of or not? If so, please choose as many responses as seem appropriate on the card:

▲
Boys' Day, 5 May. The streamers represent the carp, renowned for its determination in swimming against the current and therefore a worthy model for young Japanese.

Close-packed grave-stones in an urban cemetery. The memory of the ancestors emphasizes the continuity of Japanese society.
▼

	JAPAN %	GREAT BRITAIN %
History and cultural inheritance	53.6	65.4
Natural environment and resources	18.4	36.4
Culture and art	29.7	34.1
Religion	4.5	8.0
Sports	11.5	31.5
Science and technology	33.9	38.2
Level of education	32.3	40.2
Potential for future development	7.6	23.6
Standard of living	11.1	28.7
Social welfare	2.4	44.5
Social stability	8.3	15.1
Nothing to be proud of	13.7	9.2

Family Relationships at Work

One other aspect of "family life" in Japan is worthy of comment, and that is the continuing prevalence of family-type relationships in business, politics and other spheres of life. The traditional Japanese household was an economic unit and the core of its labour force consisted of people who were related by blood. But it also frequently contained members who were related either only very distantly to the main descent-line of the family or not at all. These non-kin members of the household were, nevertheless, firmly committed to the economic success of the household, on which they depended for their livelihood, and they were regarded by its blood-related members as equally full members of it. They were entitled to take a full part in making decisions and even to succeed to the headship of the household if they had the approval of its present head and of the family as a whole.

Even though the Japanese household has largely lost its economic functions, something of the feeling of family-type relationships seems to carry over into the modern world of business, not only in small workshops, where an employer and his men work side by side, but even in large corporations, where the ideal of "one big happy family" is not just management propaganda. This is not to say that keen rivalry between individuals for promotion, or between departments for efficient performance, are not very much in evidence. But it does mean that members of each working-group, at each level of the organization, will feel closer to and more comfortable with other members of the group than with outsiders. Socializing with workmates, in bars or at company-owned sports complexes or resort hotels, is likely to dominate one's off-duty hours. And workers are likely to welcome rather than resent the involvement of senior colleagues in matters which, in the West, would be regarded as entirely private from work, such as family disputes or the death or marriage of a family member. Thus, surveys which ask workers whether they prefer a boss "who may force one to work hard, even to the extent of sometimes bending work rules, but who shows an active concern for one's welfare in private matters outside the job" have regularly found four out of every five employees expressing such a preference. And this proportion has varied scarcely at all over the last twenty years.

WOMEN

Japanese women are most womanly — kind, gentle, youthful, pretty. But the way in which they are treated by the men has hitherto been such as might cause a pang to any generous European breast . . . for most Japanese men . . . make no secret of their disdain for the female sex . . . . With the twentieth century the 'new woman' has begun to assert herself even in Japan. Her name figures on committees; she may even be seen riding the 'bike' and more usefully employed in some of the printing offices and telephone exchanges. Such developments, however, affect but a small percentage of the nation.

(Basil Hall Chamberlain, *Japanese Things*, 1904)

Because the task of child-rearing in Japan is considered to be mainly the responsibility of the mother, it is women who generally implant in the young their most basic ideas about how boys and girls should behave. Survey evidence suggests different orders of priority in ideas about "good behaviour" for the different sexes. Whereas the major aims for boys should be to learn "not to cause trouble to others", "to get on well with friends", "to take good care of things" and "to keep promises", for girls they are "to speak politely and cultivate good manners", "to take care of themselves" and "to help with household tasks". Learning to live with others is stressed for both sexes, but for men this means curbing aggression, for women the positive development of a pleasing personality. It is also implied that men are expected to move among a large number of casual acquaintances, whereas women will tend to have fewer but more intense relationships with a far more restricted number of people.

The home-centred assumptions of growing up as a girl in Japan are also clearly shown by the extent to which the actual behaviour demanded

Bowing to every customer who uses the escalators — a test of endurance which most shop-girls apparently survive.

of boys and girls — as opposed to ideals of behaviour — varies in practice. See the table of household tasks asked of children. The mass

HOUSEHOLD TASKS ASKED OF CHILDREN
AGED 12-15

	Percentage of Boys	Percentage of Girls
Preparing meals	6	38
Clearing up after meals	13	61
Shopping	20	38
Errands	30	40
Laundry	4	23
Cleaning rooms	34	55
Cleaning outdoors	10	17
No specific help	30	9

media help to reinforce this pattern. The sort of thoughtful and unselfish behaviour expected from females in Japan can be judged from the types of advice given to readers of teenage magazines:

To be attractive a high school girl should look beautiful in her school uniform.
1. Always wear a white blouse which is well starched and ironed
2. Carry three clean handkerchiefs at all times
3. Brush and comb your hair well
4. Keep your nails clean
5. Keep dandruff off your uniform

Talk among friends is good, but anything that might offend someone in the group should be avoided. Stay off such topics as poor physical appearance of your friends, such as shortness or fatness; your father, if someone in the group has lost hers; politics and religion, because you should respect everyone's views on these matters; unpleasant things like crime and sickness. Also, do not talk about or judge people who are not present.

Young people with any common sense should not go to a park at night, a deserted area, or a dimly lit, shady tea shop.

When you want to talk about something pleasant but light, sit facing each other. When the subjects are more serious, such as romantic dreams or hopes for the future, it is better to sit side by side on a bench, for instance, so that you will not be facing each other directly.

If you must break up . . .
1. Accept the blame, even if that is not the case.
2. Do not keep him guessing. Once you have spoken to him about breaking up, stop dating completely.
3. Talk to him when he is calm.

It is not the price of a gift that matters but the feeling behind it.
Select something to match his taste or character.
It is better to choose something that will not last for ever.
Once you have given him something, it is not in good taste to keep asking him whether he is using it.
To give a white handkerchief to someone of the opposite sex means goodbye.

Marriage

The marriage rate in Japan is significantly higher than in other industrialized countries. In a number of Western European countries nearly 10% of the population remain unmarried. In Japan a bachelor is regarded as something of an oddity and a woman who remains unmarried after 25 is in danger of being referred to as "ure nokori" (literally, unsold goods). The reported desire for marriage among women increases every year between the ages of 20 and 25 and then decreases dramatically. After the age of 30 there is a marked increase in the number of those who state that they have no desire to marry.

According to a 1974 survey by the Headquarters for Youth Affairs, the percentage of people who want to marry "for love" is on the increase. 65% of unmarried females expressed the wish to find their own husbands, while only 11% "hope that someone around me will act as match-maker". But when it came to the form and style of the wedding ceremony itself, more than twice as many said that they would consider their parents' and other people's opinions than said that they

Traditional costume at the wedding ceremony — but traditional attitudes to the roles of husband and wife are changing.

would make the decision according to their own feelings. The idea that marriage is something that concerns the whole family as much as the individuals actually marrying is still very strong.

Although, in theory, many young people express themselves in favour of "love-matches", in practice, traditional customs have been extremely resistant to change. Of these the most characteristically Japanese is that of "o-miai" (literally, to see and be seen), a form of pre-arranged "chance" meeting between prospective partners at a theatre or restaurant or in a park or other public place. Such meetings are the result of lengthy and delicate investigations conducted on behalf of the parents of marriageable sons and daughters by "go-betweens", who are usually trusted friends or close relatives. The use of go-betweens enables families to screen out unsuitable candidates without giving or receiving offence.

A successful o-miai will result in regular dating and marriage within a matter of months. A girl may have as many as half a dozen o-miai arranged before deciding on a partner, but if she goes beyond that number she is likely to gain a reputation for being fussy and the parents of prospective husbands may become reluctant to allow their sons to meet her because the likelihood of a rejection is so high. Nevertheless, some parents, anxious to marry off awkward daughters, continue to arrange o-miai which the daughters, divided between filial duty and dislike of marriage, continue to attend and sabotage.

The survival of o-miai, despite radical changes in the law and public attitudes, can partly be explained by the difficulty which young Japanese can experience in meeting potential partners for a romantic relationship. Teenagers have to cope with long hours of homework and extra tuition. Young office workers must frequently commute for 3 or 4 hours a day, which leaves little time or energy for "night life" — and that, in any case, is often enjoyed in the company of office colleagues. College students enjoy freer relationships and have more time at their disposal, but most are too poor to give serious thought to marriage and relegate it, like a permanent job, to the unknown future, after graduation. It must also be remembered that the great majority of young people in Japan, including many students, continue to live at home, under their parents' supervision, until the time that they do get married and establish their own household. Casual meetings, without a formal introduction, whether they take place at parties, coffee shops or recreational facilities, are not regarded as an approved way of finding a marriage partner. Japanese also tend to feel emotionally uncomfortable at the thought of approaching strangers, and, therefore, for psychological reasons, tend to welcome, or even look for, the assistance of an intermediary.

Housewives

Most Japanese women are not geisha, air hostesses, clerks, nurses, teachers, sales assistants or farm workers. They are housewives. According to Suzanne H. Vogel, an American psychiatric social worker, we should learn to think of "housewife" as an occupational category, indeed as a career, to be understood in terms of its skills, structure and patterns of recruitment, training and retirement. Arguing that "industrialization does not automatically bring with it a Western pattern of sex roles", Ms Vogel sees in the "*sarariman*" (salary man — a white-collar, monthly-paid office-worker) a reincarnation of the samurai, dedicated to his values of discipline, loyalty and hard work. His efficient functioning depends, however, upon the untiring support of his wife. Taking care of her husband is not seen so much as servile repression, but rather as her complementary contribution to the efficiency and prosperity of the family. Like the *sarariman*, she has job security through life-time employment. And as the *sarariman* sacrifices himself to his company, so his wife sacrifices herself to her family. Ms Vogel sees in this relationship a key to understanding the wider society in which it operates:

Whereas in America the ideal man or woman is independent, self-reliant and capable of multiple roles or skills, in Japan men and women both strive toward an ideal of interdependence, division of labour and primacy of the group (whether business group or family) rather than the individual.

"A husband should be two things — healthy and at work". The home is the setting for women's recreation, while men go out on the town.

"Preparation" for the career of housewife begins in childhood, when a girl is praised and rewarded for being patient, quiet and tidy. She learns that a woman's status is derived from that of the males upon whom she depends, and that it is therefore in her own interest to bolster the confidence and reputation of her father, brothers and, eventually, her husband.

Once married, the urban, middle-class wife assumes the major responsibility for the running of the household. In four fifths of all homes it is the wife who manages the family budget, deciding what and when to save, buy and invest, and doling out a weekly allowance of "pocket money" to her apparently masterful husband. She is as likely as he is to tend the garden and see to minor household repairs and, while it is increasingly common for younger and more highly educated husbands to help out with taking care of the children or making the beds, it is still virtually unthinkable that a husband might cook, go shopping or wash dishes. Anything that the husband contributes is a bonus — or possibly even a threat to what is properly the woman's domain. A good husband, as the saying goes, should be healthy — and at work. Family problems are therefore far more likely to be blamed on the failure of the mother than on the absence of or neglect of the father.

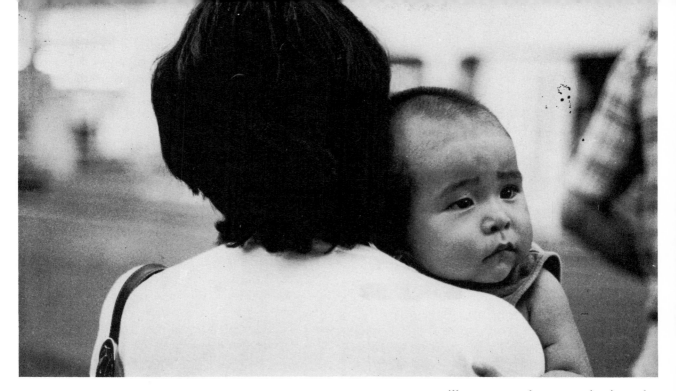

Hold on tight. A Japanese psychiatrist has argued that the strength of group-loyalties in Japanese society reflects a yearning to re-establish the absolute security of the mother-child relationship.

It is no coincidence, Suzanne Vogel asserts, that the Suzuki method of teaching the violin, which requires the mother to learn and practise with her child, originated in Japan. Devotion and discrimination in developing skills in human relations are the hallmark of Japanese womanhood. Mother and mother-in-law, magazines and TV shows, the PTA and neighbourhood gossip are all sources of "professional development" for the dedicated housewife. Through them she will learn how to choose the right sort of gifts for New Year and Mid-summer, how to cultivate good relations with her children's teachers and how to manipulate others by praise or by appearing hurt, rather than by confrontation and aggression.

According to Suzanne Vogel, the Japanese wife has a clearly defined sphere of activity and this brings with it a sense of autonomy and independence. The significance of the "professional" aspect of the housewife's role down-grades the importance of the emotional bond between husband and wife; even when warmth is lacking here,

a woman can still carry out her most basic tasks as mother and mistress of the household. Three possible crisis situations provide evidence to support this view and underline the fundamental importance of the sexual division of labour. Firstly, adultery by the wife *is* more serious than adultery by the husband, because by affecting her reputation and emotional stability, it affects her performance as mother and caretaker, whereas the man's role as financial provider and nominal head of the household is untouched by extramarital relationships. Secondly, the death of either parent precipitates the effective dissolution of the household and forces the survivor to depend on their grown-up children, in the case of men, for domestic services, and in the case of women, for the very necessities of life. And thirdly, if a man becomes mentally ill, his company invariably keeps his job open and pays his salary as usual, while his wife visits him, runs the household as usual and eventually helps him reintegrate with society. If a woman falls victim to serious mental disturbance, however, the domestic vacuum caused by her absence soon becomes intolerable and there is a high risk of her being divorced or abandoned as her husband searches for a replacement.

Ms Vogel concludes that if a Japanese woman's

status *as a wife* is lower than it is in the West, her status *as a mother* is definitely higher. Add to this the strength which comes from her expertise in running the household and one can understand why it is she, rather than the nominally all-powerful husband, who is really the pivot of the family.

This conclusion is firmly endorsed by Hara Hiraho, a Professor of Anthropology, who is also a wife and mother:

If you judge Japanese — men or women — only by their public social status, you miss the vital other half, perhaps the most important half, of Japanese life. Japanese men look down on women in many categorical ways but they do not look down on the woman's role . . .

Post-war Japan has been remarkable among industrial societies for the lowness of its divorce rate. Apart from in the immediate post-war years, a period of rapid and major social readjustment, when many women exercised their newly-acquired legal equality to rid themselves of unwanted husbands, the divorce rate remained fairly steady until 1965, at about 0.6 to 0.7 per 1000 population, less than one tenth of the marriage rate. Since 1965, Japan has tended to follow the trend in other industrialized countries and by 1975 the rate had risen to 1.0 per thousand, about one eighth of the marriage rate. This is still very low, however, when compared with other countries.

In Japan divorce is most common among those who have been married less than one year or between five and ten years (i.e. where there are young children). Almost 90% of divorces are by mutual consent and only 1% come through a court of law, the rest being handled by arbitration. Divorced women are, however, at a severe disadvantage economically. Employment opportunities for divorced women are extremely limited (they may go, for instance, into clerical work, or work as sales assistants or bar-hostesses), particularly when the woman has the responsibility of small children. Nevertheless, more than 80% of divorced women do find work of some sort, though few manage to find secure employment with a large firm. One third are self-employed or work in family businesses; most of the rest are hired on a daily or temporary basis. In such a situation a woman's best chance of economic survival depends on the willingness of parents and other relatives to assist her by providing living-space or minding the children. Divorced women tend to have below-average incomes, above-average health problems and frequent difficulties with housing and insecurity of income.

It is interesting to note that in the Meiji period, when a divorced peasant woman could return to her father's household, which was itself a productive unit, the divorce rate was three times as high as it is today. Urbanization, the trend to nuclear families and the decline in the number of family businesses have combined to strengthen the economic pressures against divorce. The tendency is further reinforced by widespread social disapproval of divorce, expressed both by men and by women. Only about 5% of the divorced and widowed remarry in Japan. In the USA 50% of divorced women remarry and so do 25% of widows.

Women at Work

Since pre-modern times women have supplied a large proportion of the labour force in agriculture, retailing and, to a lesser extent, in the handicraft industries. Since 1945 a number of factors have combined to diversify the pattern of female employment. Chief among these factors are:
1. Women's enhanced legal status and extended educational opportunities.
2. Continuing changes in technology, the rapid expansion of the economy and a rising general standard of affluence, which have stimulated the demand for skilled and educated labour in both manufacturing and the service industries.
3. Dramatic changes in the size and structure of families, both cause and consequence of newly available techniques of birth-control, which have made it increasingly feasible for women to attempt to combine the roles of wife, mother and worker.

The most important changes in the pattern of female employment since 1945 may be summarised as follows:
1. The number of women working in agriculture has fallen consistently. Nevertheless, women now provide the bulk of the nation's farm labour force.

2. The number of women working in industry and services has tripled between 1950 and 1975.

3. Whereas in 1950 61.3% of working women were employed in family businesses (farms, shops, workshops), by 1975 the percentage had fallen to 32.8. For most working women, therefore, employment now involves leaving the home and accepting the contractual status of employee, whose rights and obligations no longer depend on relatives.

4. More and more women are going back to work after their children go to school. By 1975 the proportion of women aged 40-49 at work was almost as large as of those aged 20-24.

5. Whereas in 1955 only 20.9% of women employees were married, by 1975 the percentage had risen to 51.3.

6. Part-time work (up to 30 hours a week) increased rapidly during the high-growth 1960s, when employers began to hit a labour shortage and families sought to increase their purchasing-power to share in the nation's new affluence. Between 1965 and 1975 the percentage of part-time workers who were also housewives rose from 9.4 to 17.1. Many of these have low job-security and poor working-conditions and thus form a "cushion" of easily disposable labour which can be laid off during recessions.

The increasing sophistication of modern industrial technology and the new range of responsibilities accepted by the modern welfare state have created a demand for a wide range of technical, managerial and other professional specialists. The distribution of women among these various occupational roles is extremely uneven. Virtually all nurses and kindergarten attendants are women. So are 54.5% of elementary school teachers and 51.4% of pharmacists. But only 5.5% of managerial posts are held by women. Women account for only 10.2% of doctors and dentists, 5.1% of scientific research workers and 2.5% of lawyers and judges.

Because large-scale organizations in Japan base promotions on the principles of life-time employment and seniority, women workers who wish to break the continuity of their career to have children are necessarily at a disadvantage. Because employers normally expect to recruit workers for life and are thus willing to bear the cost of their training, they are reluctant to recruit workers who cannot fit this pattern, or they are reluctant, having recruited them, to give them the training which might qualify them for promotion. But basic assumptions about the "proper" roles of men and women, and their inherent natures and abilities are also significant factors. As Kyoko Bernard notes:

> The vast majority of men and women consider it harmful for the development of children to have a mother with a full-time job. This attitude which is subscribed to most rigidly by the male element of the population with a university education together with housewives in general, contributes to label a career woman with a family as automatically being a bad mother and wife.

Women are also less well-paid than men. Although starting salaries for women and men are roughly comparable, differentials grow much wider within a few years — from about 10% at

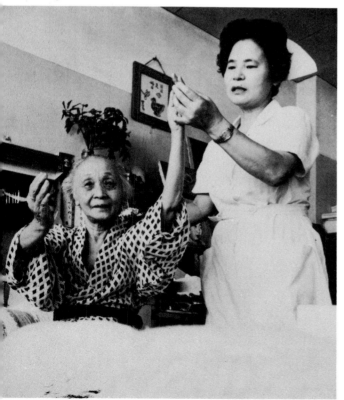

Women are prominent in the "caring professions" — and among those in need of care.

age 25 to as much as 50% at age 45. Japanese wage systems are structured around the needs of male employees who are assumed to be heads of households. Women's wages are therefore regarded as supplementary to a household income, and this works to the disadvantage of single and divorced women wholly dependent on their own earning power.

Women and Politics

Public opinion surveys reveal that two thirds of all Japanese consider women to be not politically minded. Behavioural analysis confirms the reality of this impression:

Self Expressed Interest in Politics	% Men	% Women
Very interested	11	3
Considerably interested	32	13
Somewhat interested	44	54
Almost no interest	12	28

Although there appears to be no relationship between women's high level of electoral participation and their low level of political awareness and involvement in policy-making, women are greatly involved in the activities of a wide range of voluntary organizations, based on regions, religions, trade unions and local communities. In recent years women have played an increasingly prominent part in the many "citizen's movements" ("*jumin undo*") which have grown up on an ad hoc basis to campaign for consumers' rights and environmental protection and against political corruption and the development of nuclear power.

The most politically active women tend to be in their 30s, probably because, as housewives, they have a certain amount of leisure time, and, as mothers with young children, they are especially aware of educational and welfare issues and the environmental hazards created by traffic and pollution. Taketsugu Tsurutani, a leading political scientist, has suggested that "issue-oriented" politics, in which the main combatants are temporary associations rather than permanent political parties, may be the predominant mode of political conflict in "post-industrial" societies where affluence has been achieved and the

"quality of life" becomes the central concern of public policy. If this is so, we can expect women's role in Japanese politics to become increasingly important.

Women Today

Susan Pharr, an American sociologist, suggests that younger Japanese women (under 35) today can be divided into three major categories — "Neotraditionalists", "New Women" and "Radical Egalitarians". The great majority of Japanese women are, according to Ms Pharr, still "Neotraditionalists"; that is to say, they still believe strongly in their roles as wives and mothers. All other claims on their time and emotional and intellectual resources must be subordinated to the demands of home and family. Nevertheless, the Neotraditionalists do deserve the epithet "Neo", for they are not mere reincarnations of pre-war womanhood. For them, the "normal" progression of the life cycle now includes both secondary (and possibly higher) education and a period of paid employment.

"New Women", however, do more than merely progress through phases of higher education and paid employment. Many would make these stepping-stones to a full-fledged career. Yet New Women are not eager to renounce marriage and motherhood. Rather they seek to reconcile the roles of wife and mother with the desire to participate in a wider world.

"Radical Egalitarians" are members of a tiny minority who reject not merely traditional conceptions of marriage but the entire ethos of Japanese society and its institutions — the state, business, the education system, etc. Opting out of the conventional life-style, they turn either to political activism, usually with a Marxist affiliation, or to militant feminism, with the stress on sexual freedom. In Ms Pharr's words, the views of the Radical Egalitarians go "far beyond what most Japanese men and women can even understand, much less accept".

Ms Pharr foresees tensions and changes arising for all three categories and in their relationship with one another. Neotraditionalists are facing a crisis of meaninglessness as houses and families become smaller and less time-consuming. They may also find that prolonged education, which they undertake merely to bolster their marriage "credentials", can have unexpected results and plant the first seeds of discontent. Several powerful social forces appear to favour the diffusion of New Women aspirations — secure prosperity, growing contact with Western values and the spread of higher education. But the realization of these aspirations is likely to be frustrated by the uncomprehending attitude of Japanese political and labour leaders and the unsatisfying nature of the employment currently available to women. The Radical Egalitarians are so far out of sympathy with the mass of Japanese women as to be effectively confined to their own self-made sub-culture. Widespread frustration among New Women might, however, provide them with an audience which they have so far sought in vain.

EDUCATION

. . . they are most eager to extend the bounds of their knowledge in the arts and sciences . . . .
(Edinburgh Review, 1852)

From its Confucian past, Japan has inherited a tradition of respect for learning and the learned man. (University professors are popular TV pundits in Japan.) Economic modernization and the growth of democracy have so intensified and generalized the desire for education that it can be said to have become virtually a national obsession.

The Education System

That the Japanese education system has some formidable achievements to its credit cannot be denied. Despite the need to master a fiendishly difficult writing system, the proportion of illiterates in Japan is reckoned at less than half of one

PERCENTAGE OF RELEVANT AGE-GROUP
IN HIGHER EDUCATION

Year	Senior High School	University
1955	51.5	10.1
1960	57.7	10.3
1965	70.7	17.0
1970	82.1	23.6
1975	91.9	37.8
1980	94.2	37.4

First steps on the educational escalator — a well-equipped primary school classroom.

"Space Invaders" — a Japanese invention and craze.
Teenage boys playing in an amusement parlour.

per cent of the adult population. A basic familiarity with the vocabulary of science is widespread, as is the ability to read music. Truancy from schools is virtually unknown. Teachers are respected and relatively well-paid. The absence of "streaming" and the universal acceptance of a common curriculum mean that only a tiny minority of children are treated as "unteachable" and the vast majority of the people share a culture in which class, regional and religious distinctions are insignificant. Apart from anything else, this means that when parents' work obliges them to move from one part of the country to another, the disruption in their children's schooling is kept to a minimum. Another factor which assists in this and illustrates the emphasis on equality of educational provision is that there are no major inequalities between different parts of the country when it comes to teacher-pupil ratios, teacher qualifications or the provision of equipment and facilities.

Even the fact that teachers and pupils both take part in cleaning chores at school helps to ensure that menial tasks are not despised. Home—school contacts are also close, even though most Japanese teachers have forty or more pupils in their classes. Poor work, inconsiderate behaviour or indulgence in forbidden activities, such as smoking, are met with clear and early disapproval, both at school and in the home. Actual punishment is rarely needed and the vast majority of students grow up to be diligent, well-mannered and co-operative.

William K. Cummings, an American educationalist, argues that:

> The emphasis in the Japanese school on moral education is perhaps its most outstanding characteristic. It is responsible for a wide variety of other educational and social outcomes; the orderliness of the classroom and of society . . . and the unity and cohesiveness of the Japanese nation . . . . Moral education in the Japanese school is not simply another course in the curriculum . . . . School assemblies, excursions, school events, daily lunches and an array of other . . . activities serve as vehicles for achieving moral education.

Public interest in education in Japan is constantly stimulated by the well-publicized tension between the Ministry of Education, which exer-

Baseball practice. Sport must be fitted into a crowded
curriculum and a crowded landscape.

cises detailed control over syllabuses and text-
books, and the Japan Teachers' Union, to which
about three quarters of all teachers belong. The
Ministry tends to reflect the outlook of the government and business elite, which sees education
as an instrument for promoting social stability
and producing a skilled and highly-motivated
work-force. The JTU emphasizes the importance
of education as a means towards developing well-
balanced personalities with critical and enquiring
minds, who will become not merely conscientious
workers and public-spirited neighbours but, if
need be, determined protesters as well.

Japanese education, whatever its virtues and
successes, has seemed to many observers to merit
all too well the catch-phrase description "examination hell". A 1971 report by the Organization
for Economic Co-operation and Development
noted sternly that:

An emphasis on selection rather than on the
development of the innate abilities of the

student occurs at practically all levels of
education. This tendency seems to be, to a
large extent, the result . . . of the system of
university entrance examinations . . . . This
distorts much of the education which takes
place before this age, as well as that which
follows later.

Entry to a prestigious university has been a virtual guarantee of well-paid and secure employment in post-war Japan. While parents pay lip-
service to the ideal of a balanced education with
due attention to art, sport and music, in practice
they have tended to drive their children to con-
centrate all their energies on academic work.
And whereas in Britain and the USA children go
to school for an average of 180 days a year, in
Japan the figure is 240. Two hours of homework a
night is normal from the age of 11 or 12 onwards,
and some two thirds of all high-school students
also attend a "*juku*" or "cramming school" two
or three times a week in the evenings or at weekends. The pressure is intense and everybody
knows it. And the results do not always impress.

The "*soroban*", the Japanese abacus, which children learn to master in primary school.

In the opinion of an English professor at the renowned International Christian University, the Japanese education system, despite its emphasis on rote-learning and accurate memorization "is hardly concerned with education content. Its function is to develop *attitudes* not skills or intelligence and least of all imagination or a spirit of enquiry".

Even Professor Vogel, arch-enthusiast of Japanese achievements, is forced to admit that when it comes to universities, the shortcomings are many and obvious:

> . . . faculty devotion to teaching and to students is limited . . . analytic rigour in the classroom is lacking and attendance is poor. University expenditures per student are unreasonably low and the level and variety of advanced research are highly limited.

Considerable inequalities can also be said to persist in the educational experience of the two sexes, despite the fact that co-education has become the norm since the war. Two thirds of the girls in higher education are enrolled in two-year junior college diploma courses, rather than in four-year university degree courses. And even in the universities their enrolment is very unevenly distributed between different faculties. Home economics has a 99% female intake and pharmacology, education and the liberal arts all have above 60%, whereas less than 10% of the students in agriculture or engineering are female.

Despite the rapid expansion of educational opportunities for women in the post-war period, the nature of that education and the social and occupational roles for which it is an adequate preparation have been constrained by long-established social attitudes about women's abilities and their place in society. According to a 1976 survey, 57% of Japanese parents wished to see their sons go to university, but only 25% felt the same about their daughters. Another survey conducted in the same year revealed that 66% of people questioned hoped that their sons would acquire the qualifications necessary to enter a

School uniform is worn almost everywhere and without protest.

specialized profession, while wishing that their daughters should become "happy family women".

Adult Education

Whatever else the Japanese may or may not acquire as a result of their experience of education, they do seem to retain a voracious appetite for knowledge and a tireless willingness to study. Japanese television offers a very high proportion of educational programmes, including regular courses on English, French, German, Russian and Chinese, and special series to meet the needs of farmers, small businessmen and mothers of young children. Intellectual periodicals are both more numerous and more widely read than in Britain or America and the level of all the mass-circulation newspapers is "serious". Adult education courses are offered not only by universities but by companies, local communities and even department stores. Employees of large corporations are almost bound, as a matter of course, to become members of study-groups several times in the course of their careers.

Hitachi, Japan's largest heavy electrical company, puts all its recruits through a two-year basic training programme. Like many companies, it stresses the need for employees to learn the business from all angles. Even graduate engineers must spend their first six months in blue-collar jobs. Fujitsu, the country's biggest computer manufacturer, starts training recruits six months *before* they officially start with the company and offers its mid-career managers lectures on Western literature so that they can converse with foreigners as the company becomes increasingly international.

As in so many other aspects of national life, the example has come from the state itself. Ever since the Iwakura mission of 1871 took the cream of Japan's leaders on a two-year study tour of the West, successive governments have selected teams of bright young men to learn from abroad. When they return they are expected to keep up their reading. As Professor Vogel puts it, "bureaucrats consider no responsibility greater than keeping well-informed".

What is true of government is also true of big business. As a senior executive of C. Itoh and Co., the third biggest of Japan's "Sogo Shosha" (trading companies), declares, "the most important function of our company today is processing information. We undertake the necessary investigations to keep trade flowing." An opposite number at Marubeni Corporation, which ranks just behind C. Itoh and Co., has explained that:

Our overseas branches have teams of specialists with a thorough knowledge of the market and a command of the language of the country.

On top of all this the offices are linked by extensive computer networks. Sogo Shosha have the reputation of being among the few organisations in the world other than governments with information networks on this scale.

Mitsui and Co., the biggest of them all, has more than 200 offices world-wide, connected with headquarters by more than a quarter of a million miles of transmission lines, along which pass some 30 million messages a year. Like most Japanese, this giant corporation has no need to be convinced of the old truth that "knowledge is power".

RELIGION

They are not religious in sentiment but devout worshippers in practice.

The Japanese are not a religious people — except when they are. Neither in terms of the wealth they control, nor of the personnel they employ, nor of the political influence they wield, can religious organizations be said to play a particularly prominent part in Japan today. The contrast is striking, not only with countries, such as Burma, Thailand, India, Pakistan or Iran, but also with Western countries, such as Italy, Spain or Ireland. The Japanese constitution states quite clearly that:

No religious organization shall receive any privileges from the State, nor exercise any political authority. No person shall be compelled to take part in any religious act, celebration, rite or practice. The State and its organs shall refrain from religious education or any other religious activity.

And the Japanese man in the street will, if questioned about the part religion plays in his life, probably say that it plays little or none at all — though this is less likely to be true for the woman in the street or the old person of either sex, particularly if the street happens to be in a village rather than a big city.

But if religion shapes neither the structure of society nor the pattern of daily life, it remains true that the overwhelming majority of Japanese

Individual prayer is a frequent response to crisis or anticipated problems.

Festivals are colourful, noisy and cheerful.

still take part, at least nominally, in the religious observances associated with New Year's Day and the O-Bon summer festival, and in local shrine festivals, and that rites of passage through birth, marriage and death are also marked by priestly rituals.

Japanese religion, like so many other aspects of the national culture, is a mixture of indigenous elements and imported beliefs and practices which have been "Japanized" over the course of the centuries. Most people subscribe to both of the country's two main religious traditions — Shinto and Buddhism — and see no contradiction in doing so. Christianity's exclusivism, which forbids the believer simultaneous membership of another faith, has often been cited as a major reason for its failure to gain ground in a country which has in so many other ways been eager and willing to adopt foreign ideals and values.

Shinto is the native cult of Japan, originating in its earliest history and bound up with the myths of its divine creation. Shinto has no foun-

der, no congregational act of worship, and no formal scriptures as such. An official Japanese government pamphlet describes Shinto as a combination of "native worship, tribal cult, hero worship and reverence of the Emperor". No specific code of ethics is associated with it, though it stresses reverence for the beauty and majesty of nature, expresses joy in fertility and abundance, abhorrence at the defilement of blood and death, and respect for the inherent goodness of a sincere heart. Emotional rather than intellectual, expressed through rituals rather than creeds, the "way of the gods" remains unique to the land of its birth and still plays its part on ceremonial occasions.

Buddhism came to Japan via China, a thousand years after it was first preached in India. Adopted at first by the imperial court, it spread only slowly through the rest of society, developing many different forms as it did so. Its seven main branches in Japan have given birth to more than 100 sects. Among the samurai warriors the austere teachings of Zen, with their emphasis on self-discipline, found much favour. Among the common people sects which offered personal salvation through prayer and dramatic rituals gained a wide following. Buddhism also had a profound influence on the arts, especially painting, pottery, sculpture and poetry.

Christianity, introduced to Japan by Jesuit and other missionaries in the sixteenth century, at first made rapid progress, but was then stamped out by the government, which feared that an alien faith might lead to political subversion. Re-introduced when Japan opened itself again to foreign influences in the nineteenth century, it has failed to make much headway, in spite of vigorous missionary efforts, especially by American Protestants. However, Japan's one million Christians do exert influence out of all proportion to their numbers in intellectual and charitable fields.

Christianity has also made its mark in another way, clearly influencing the organization, and to some extent the forms of worship, of the so-called "New Religions" which have appeared in Japan over the last century and a half and especially since the last war. In their doctrines and rituals these "new religions" are largely re-statements of Shinto and Buddhist traditions, but, unlike the long-established religious organizations, the more recent movements have directly confronted present-day problems of family break-ups, juvenile delinquency, career difficulties and many other outcomes of personal frustration and despair. Most emphasize that health, happiness, prosperity and peace are not only important but can be achieved by a combination of faith and effort. Their recruits have often been those whose lives have been disrupted by the great forces which have changed Japanese society — industrialization, urbanization and defeat. The most notable of these movements is probably the "Soka Gakkai" or "Value-Creating Society", which promotes a reformed and rather nationalistic form of Buddhism with evangelical fervour and methods, and which supports not only its own newspaper and publishing house, but also its own university and symphony orchestra, and which even founded its own political party — the "Komeito", or "Clean Government Party", though this has now severed its formal links with Soka Gakkai. By organizing members in small

Buddhist monks at meditation. Zen practices have attracted many Westerners.

groups, where they can help each other with day-to-day problems, and by arranging spectacular mass rallies from time to time, Soka Gakkai and similar organizations can give their members a sense of belonging to a movement which is both intimate and caring and immensely powerful.

Neither Shinto nor Japanese Buddhism have stressed ethical obligations. In Japan these have been derived from China's Confucian tradition and seen as something set apart from, but no less important than, religious observances. A Japanese intellectual explained a hundred years ago that

morals were invented by the Chinese because they were an immoral people; but in Japan there was no necessity for any system of morals, as every Japanese acted aright if he only consulted his own heart.

This elaborate Buddha in the eleventh-century Byodoin ▶
(Phoenix Hall) near Nara attests to the profound influence of religion on the arts in Japan.

CRIME

Their justice is severely executed without any partiality upon transgressors of the law. They are governed in great civility. I mean, not a land better governed in the world by civil policy.

(William Adams, 1611)

Between 1946 and 1973 crime in Japan, measured in terms of offences reported, arrests made and persons convicted, declined by roughly a half. The chaotic conditions and extreme poverty of the immediate post-war period created a brief crime-wave which was brought under control as prosperity returned and war-torn communities gradually re-established a more stable way of life. Western observers, puzzled by the growth in crime in their own societies even as they became visibly wealthier and more tolerant year after year, were even more puzzled to see that Japan seemed to be immune from this trend.

Since the early 1970s the overall level of criminal activities appears to have stabilized, but in a number of areas the persistence and, in some cases, the growth of criminal behaviour have continued to give the authorities cause for concern. Of these, the drug problem is probably the greatest. Between 1969 and 1979 the number of people arrested for the abuse of stimulant drugs rose by more than 25 times. Thefts and traffic accidents involving drug addicts also increased dramatically and it was estimated that by the beginning of the 1980s drug trafficking accounted for more than half of the income of organized criminal gangs. More alarming still was the sense that the problem was even bigger than these figures suggested. The 1980 White Paper issued by the National Police Agency admitted that "there are now possibly about ten times as many unidentified addicts as those arrested".

Drug users appear to be most commonly those whose work involves constant effort or tension over long hours: migrant building workers, restaurant workers and small business owners seem to be especially vulnerable.

Other areas of crime singled out by the National Police Agency as especially problematic are:
(a) insurance and credit card frauds
(b) the rising number of juveniles involved in crime — typical crimes include traffic violations by motorcycle gangs, attacks on teachers by pupils and glue sniffing.
(c) "guerilla" attacks and violent demonstrations by left-wing and right-wing political extremists.

Nevertheless, in comparison with the other major industrial democracies, Japan remains a remarkably law-abiding nation, as the table shows.

CRIME RATE PER 100,000 INHABITANTS (1981)

	Homicide	Rape	Robbery
USA	9.8	35.6	250.6
England and Wales	2.4	7.2	36.3
Japan	1.5	2.2	2.0

TOTAL ARRESTS PER 100 OFFENCES

USA	71.6	48.1	23.9
England and Wales	82.6	89.6	24.7
Japan	97.4	89.3	81.5

How can Japan's relative success in controlling crime be explained? Two main factors seem to be important — the professionalism of the police and the attitude of the public.

The Police

Entrants to the Japanese police are carefully selected and their educational standard compares favourably with that of the population as a whole. Initial training lasts for at least a year. A policeman is expected to be at all times as courteous as he is self-confident. Pride in the force is strengthened by sports and social activities, such as judo and kendo clubs, and by the knowledge that the public trusts and respects policemen and that policemen are given considerable freedom in handling particular incidents. Where policemen feel that a word with an offender, his family or neighbours will be more appropriate than a fine or imprisonment, they know that their superiors will back their judgment.

Law enforcement in Japan benefits from a virtuous circle of success. Because the crime level is lower, police have more time to pursue each enquiry. The result is a much higher clear-up rate than in the USA or UK. In cases of robbery, rape, murder, arson and embezzlement, the culprits are arrested in four cases out of five. The virtual certainty of detection is a powerful deterrent to further crime and thus keeps the crime rate low.

Punishment is relatively lenient. Juvenile offenders are frequently dismissed with a severe talking-to — the first time. Most never come back for a second, knowing full well that they have brought shame not only on themselves but on their families and schools as well. What are sometimes called "crimes without victims", such as drunkenness and prostitution, are rarely the subject of police intervention, unless violence is involved. Prison is a last resort, for adults as well as for juveniles. Of the 2,186,000 people sentenced in 1979 over 95% were fined and only 3.5% sentenced to prison; and 60% of those sentenced to prison for a first offence had their sentence suspended. In 1978 in the USA there were 121 people in prison for every 100,000 persons. The comparable figure for the UK was 85, for Japan 43. It is also striking that there are more than 17 times as many lawyers per head of the population in the USA than in Japan. A 1980 Opinion Survey suggests that the Japanese public would support a much tougher line against criminals. A majority of the population supports the death penalty and believes that its abolition would lead to an increase in serious crimes. 90% of respondents to the survey also approved strict measures against drug trafficking.

"Community policing" — a road safety lesson at school.

Relations between police and public are close and cordial. The high density of population means that most Japanese are no more than a few minutes from one of the 15,000 police sub-stations which are spread across the country. The average response time for a call on the emergency telephone number, "110", is just over three minutes. Police have all the latest modern equipment, but still rely heavily on foot and bicycle patrols, and on getting to know the people of the locality. Noticeboards outside police sub-stations are used for posting local announcements. Giving first-aid, directing strangers and finding lost property are regarded as normal daily activities.

Each household is expected to register all residents with the local police, together with details of regular over-night visitors, motor-vehicles and other valuable items. This enables police to check up on strangers or trace stolen property easily and quickly. Japanese do not regard giving such information as an invasion of privacy but rather as a sensible precaution. In every village and neighbourhood there is also a local crime prevention association to help the police keep up to date on local happenings and to spread information from the police to local people. Over the years the police have come to expect the trust and co-operation of the public, and the public have come to expect that the police will be honest, competent, sympathetic but relentless. This sort of relationship still seems to be found in small communities in the USA and Britain. But in Japan it is found in the big cities as well — yet further evidence of the Japanese ability to maintain in modern circumstances the most positive aspects of a more traditional way of life.

TIME OFF

The people . . . are well dressed, prosperous and are much given to continual recreations, amusements and pastimes, such as going on picnics to enjoy the sight of the flowers and gardens.

(Joao Rodrigues S.J., ca. 1600)

Leisure, like practically every other human activity in Japan, has been subjected to exhaustive analysis, and the results of the many surveys that have been undertaken reveal a great deal more about the Japanese than merely how to spend an idle hour in Tokyo.

Leisure patterns are clearly related to generation differences. There appears to be a significant division between the over-40s, who can remember the hard times of the 1930s, the war years and the Occupation, and the under-40s, whose lifetime experience is of a rising and seemingly permanent prosperity. Whereas the older generation still tend to work overtime most days, go in to work six days a week and take only a fraction of their annual holiday entitlement, younger Japanese are much more likely to take off all the time they are entitled to. Generation differences are reflected not only in amounts of leisure time but also in the types of leisure activities preferred. Not surprisingly, older people prefer less taxing pastimes, such as gardening and handicrafts. While a minority of young people are choosing more and more strenuous and individualistic sports, such as athletics and mountaineering, an even larger proportion are opting for painting or

"Bunraku", a traditional form of puppet theatre.

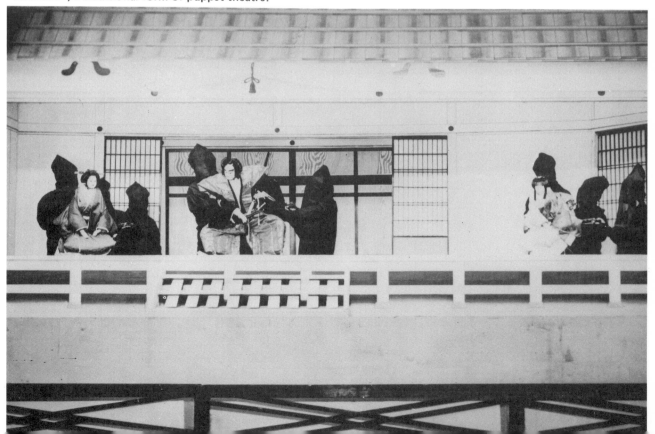

"Easterns", rather than Westerns, dominate film and TV drama.

playing a musical instrument. According to the Tokyo Foreign Press Centre,

> the cultivation of artistic sentiments among the young today is at a level incomparably higher than before. Today's younger Japanese generation thus can be expected to become equipped with the ability to enjoy leisure when they grow old at a level far above today's elderly generation.

Perhaps.

In a crowded country like Japan, lack of space necessarily imposes a major constraint on leisure activities. Hard-surface games like volley-ball and tennis can be serviced more economically than soft-surface sports like rugby or soccer, where intensive use can destroy the pitch. Golf attracts some 12 million would-be participants, but prohibitive fees confine most to routine exercises on multi-storey driving ranges. Yacht manufacturers estimate that they could sell a million boats in the 1980s; but if they were all to be berthed properly, port facilities would have to be built at seven times the average rate for the last century. Even informal leisure space is tightly restricted. The average Londoner has access to nearly twenty times as much park-space per head as the average inhabitant of Tokyo. Activities that do not depend

PARK SPACE IN MAJOR CITIES

	Square metres per person
London	22.8
New York	19.2
Paris	8.4
Nagoya	3.5
Kyoto	2.2
Osaka	1.9
Tokyo	1.4

on extensive playing areas therefore attract the

most participants, and the space factor goes a long way towards explaining the popularity of sports such as swimming, angling, hiking, baseball, table tennis, badminton and bowling.

Improved Communications

The growth of leisure has necessarily involved the development of better communications, such as the *"Shinkansen"* ("bullet train"). The service from Tokyo to Osaka, the nation's second city, opened in 1964. Within ten years this service alone was carrying up to three quarters of a million passengers in a single day. The overall growth in *Shinkansen* traffic has been spectacular:

Number of passengers carried

1964	11,018,141
1968	65,902,831
1973	128,079,908

Another important development has been the building of new roads, such as the Tomei Expressway, opened in 1961. By 1974 this single route had been used by no less than 380 million vehicles.

Domestic airline services and coastal ferries have also been significant in a country which is both mountainous and fragmented into many small islands. Between 1968 and 1974 the number of people travelling on internal flights nearly tripled as did the number of vehicles using car ferries.

Nature

The Japanese love of natural beauty is proverbial and clearly evident in their art and poetry. According to a survey conducted by the Prime Minister's Office, almost a quarter of day-trippers named "enjoying nature" as their major objective.

Under the guidance of the Environment Agency, a number of long "Natural Paths" have been laid out to join together the various national parks between Tokyo and Osaka, as well as in the southern island of Kyushu and along different stretches of coastline. And in 1973 work began on the construction of a 1,200-kilometre bicycle road along the Pacific coastline of Honshu, the main island.

Japan has 27 designated national parks, occupying some 2 million hectares (over 5% of the total area of the country), and 49 "quasi-national parks", occupying another one million hectares.

Japan's varied climate does have some advantages.

There are also 57 designated hot springs, 48 "Travellers' Villages for Youth", 14 "Workers' Villages for Rest", 55 "Forest Villages", 587 youth hostels and more than 300 publicly sponsored "People's Hotels" at famous natural beauty spots.

Baseball

In terms of numbers of spectators, baseball, which has been played in Japan for more than a century, is the nation's number one sport. Except for Hiroshima, all the teams are sponsored by business organizations, such as railways, newspapers and food companies. The high spot of the season comes in October, when the winners of the two professional leagues meet in a seven-match play-off. During the mid-season break there is also a three-match series between two all-star teams, one selected from each league. There are also two national high school tournaments each year and an annual match between two of Japan's oldest universities, Waseda and Keio.

Traditional Pastimes

Technology affects every aspect of modern life and leisure is no exception to this generalization. While *"pachinko"* (pinball) remains a national passion, with more than 30 million fans, "Space Invaders" and other electronic games, which were invented in Japan, have also gained a cult following, especially among the young. However, the rise of technology has not driven out tradition. In Japan it seldom does. Among girls, tea-ceremony, flower-arranging and the art of making kimono are still popular, for all are still regarded as desirable aspects of *"okeikogoto"*, the process of training to be a bride, which naturally involves the development of such qualities as aesthetic judgment and manual dexterity. Many women who have been introduced to these pastimes in their youth take a renewed interest in them when they are in their 30s and 40s and no longer have the responsibility of a young family. Knitting, sewing, cookery and embroidery are also popular. And the fact that so many women are interested in improving their skills suggests that, in an age of ready-made clothes and convenience foods, these activities should no longer be reckoned as "accomplishments" but rather as pastimes.

Among men, traditional-style *"sumo"* wrestling still commands a large following. The rules are simple, but the techniques are much more subtle than they might seem to the uninitiated. Punching, kicking, hair-pulling and gouging are forbidden. The object is simply to force one's opponent to touch the surface of the 5.5-metre ring with any part of his body except his feet, or else to push or throw him outside it altogether. Sumo wrestlers average around 300 pounds in weight and live on a special diet. Their large bellies make them seem gross and fat to Westerners but, in fact, they are highly muscled. Promising youngsters start at around 15 years of age and usually retire in their early 30s. Six 15-day tournaments are held each year — three in Tokyo and one each in Osaka, Nagoya and Fukuoka.

Women's Leisure

Women have not shared equally in the "leisure boom" with the men. Although they may have more hours to themselves, the time is broken up by the demands of household chores and domestic responsibilities, such as taking children to and from school. Women's access to leisure is also restricted by the fact that they have less "pocket money" than men, are less likely to be able to drive and are reluctant to leave their children in the care of others. Much "spare time" is also absorbed in helping children with their homework and attending meetings of Parent-Teachers Associations and of various women's organizations concerned with consumer affairs, community projects or religious activities. This may help to explain why the most popular leisure activity for women is watching television. According to NHK, the Japan Broadcasting Corporation, the average Japanese housewife spends 4 hours 51 minutes a day watching TV. The most popular programmes are chat-shows, quizzes and family dramas. Women also tend to spend less time than men reading books and magazines. Much of their reading is done by men as they commute to and from work.

The dominance of such passive, home-centred activities as watching TV suggests that most Japanese women cannot take advantage of the wide

◄ *Pachinko* — a national cult.

55

range of leisure activities which are available to them in theory. In the words of the report by the Research Council on Women's Problems on the *Status of Women in Modern Japan*: "despite the oft-publicized advent of the leisure era, leisure has not become a reality for women today". As the American sociologist Susan Pharr has noted:

> What many Japanese men describe as a life of leisure enjoyed by the modern wife can from another point of view be seen as a life of boredom, personal inertia and considerable loneliness. Women's magazines today reveal the other side of the picture in articles dealing with how a wife can make herself look more attractive as a way of luring her husband home from the office on time, how to prepare meals such as stews that can simmer for hours and be ready whenever a husband happens to return, and hobbies to fill the housewife's long hours at home; other articles describe how to put idle time to good use by helping children with homework.

Go — a sophisticated board game of pure strategy. ▶

Leisure is Good for You

Another significant factor in the development of leisure in post-war Japan has been a change in public attitudes. The idea that leisure pursuits are a waste of time and money has been undermined by the belief, on the part of employers, that active and satisfying leisure pursuits can help to raise workers' morale and productivity, and by the belief, on the part of the workers, that leisure activities can contribute to improving one's personal health. Some 20 million Japanese indulge in — or subject themselves to — jogging, and an even higher proportion (about one in three of the whole population) engage in some form of gymnastics, either Western-style callisthenics or the more gentle art of *Tai-Chi*. The martial arts are enjoying something of a revival after a period of disfavour during the immediate post-war period. Japanese fencing ("*kendo*" — "the way of the sword") seems likely to spread well beyond Japan, as *judo* ("the way of gentleness") did a generation ago. Nevertheless, in terms of the number of active participants, these sports

Tourism is well-developed within Japan.

are less popular than cycling, ice-skating, camping, basketball, soccer or roller-skating.

Travel

With more leisure time and spare cash and easier access to transport, the Japanese are more inclined to travel as a form of recreation. Visiting hot springs and shrines is especially popular among the older people, while those of working age are more likely to go to festivals and historic sites or to go on company-sponsored tours. Viewing cherry-blossom in the spring is a tradition which shows no sign of weakening. There is also a strong desire, especially among young people, to travel abroad.

Groups of Japanese tourists have now become a common sight in London and other European capitals, but the most favoured tourist areas for the Japanese are still those nearest to Japan itself — especially Hawaii, South Korea, Hong Kong and the Philippines. Although the number of Japanese travelling overseas tripled in the 1970s, the high cost of air fares still puts a foreign holiday beyond the reach of most people.

Passive Pastimes

It would be misleading to imply that the Japanese are constantly engaged in absorbing and self-improving sports and pastimes, which demand hours of dedicated effort. Many opt for rather self-indulgent forms of relaxation. One survey showed that "drinking alcohol" is the most popular single leisure "activity" among adult males. Other high-ranking passive pastimes include, in order, listening to recorded music, going to the cinema, watching professional sport, and going to concerts, exhibitions and museums. Playing card-games, mah-jong (a Chinese gambling game), shogi (Japanese chess) and go (a traditional board game) are popular with people of all ages and both sexes.

Leisure Industries

Whatever form it takes, leisure in Japan is becoming big business. By 1970 the gross income of the leisure industries was worth almost as much as that of the steel and motor industries put together. Leisure expenditures in 1980 were estimated to be worth ¥ 33,000 million (about £75,000 million), almost one sixth up on 1979 and eight times larger than the 1965 figure. The projected figure for 1990 is ¥ 117,000 million, nearly four times the 1980 figure. Will this be enough to change the image of the Japanese as a "nation of workaholics"?

FOREIGNERS

The Japanese are very ambitious of honours and distinctions and think themselves superior to all nations . . . . They are very polite to each other, but not to foreigners, whom they utterly despise.

(St Francis Xavier, 1552)

"I'm going to make a very blunt statement: the Japanese don't consider foreigners to be human beings" — Takamura Kenichi, author of 200 books and celebrated TV pundit, likes to be

provocative. But this allegation, made in the September 1981 edition of PHP magazine, an international journal printed in English but produced in Japan, seems to have been even more provocative than most. According to Takamura, the Japanese "don't recognise the trouble they are giving the outside world". He offers his own explanation: "It's not that we despise or wish to demean foreigners — the main reason for this feeling among the Japanese lies in the fact that we have not intermarried." This is certainly true. Japan has been isolated for most of its history and never suffered a foreign invasion until the Americans landed in 1945. Marriage between

A Japanese technician gives expert instruction in the use of agricultural machinery as part of Japan's foreign aid programme.

If the option is not eating at all, the visitor can learn to master chopsticks quite quickly.

Japanese and non-Japanese is still a very rare occurrence.

But is the basic allegation true? Some commentators have made a similar point, but less crudely, saying that when Japanese travel abroad they experience other countries and peoples as though they were a form of theatre — realistic, but somehow not quite real. Others deny it altogether. According to Edward Foy, an American Professor of English literature and long-time resident of Japan, when a prestigious Italian opera company came on tour every seat was sold out, despite sky-high prices — "If they didn't think we were humans, they wouldn't respect these things."

The relationship between Japanese and Westerners has always been bedevilled by problems arising from differences of life-style and language, which reflect more profound differences in the way that cultural traditions with separate origins conceive and express basic ideas about man, nature and society. In the late sixteenth century, soon after Europeans first came to Japan, the Jesuit Alessandro Valignano wrote that:

They have rites and ceremonies so different from those of all other nations that it seems they deliberately try to be unlike any other people. The things which they do in this respect are beyond imagining and it may truly be said that Japan is a world the reverse of Europe.

The exasperation was certainly a two-way matter, as the following incident, recorded by St Francis Xavier, well illustrates:

The Japanese way of writing is very different from ours because they write from the top of the page down to the bottom. I asked Paul [a Japanese convert] why they did not write in our way and he asked me why we did not write in their way.

Nevertheless, the Japanese showed themselves eager to learn from the strangers. As Xavier reported back to his superiors in Rome:

In general they are all so insatiable of information and so importunate in their questions that there is no end either to their arguments with us, or to their talking over our answers among themselves.

Japan's flirtation with the West lasted less than a century. Fearful that the spread of Christianity might lead to political disorders, the ruling Tokugawa family banned the alien faith and closed the country off from foreign contacts for two centuries. While Japan marked time, the West industrialized and when, in 1853, Western warships demanded that Japan open itself to trade, the Japanese had no option but to agree. To preserve its independence, Japan chose to import from the West the technology and institutions which were the basis of power in the modern world. The slogan of the day was "wakon yosai" — "Japanese spirit and Western means". The reforming emperor Meiji expressed the spirit of the times allusively, in a cryptic poem:

In my garden
Side by side
Native plants, foreign plants
Growing together

The chrysanthemum, national symbol and badge of the imperial family.

One of his leading ministers, Ito Hirobumi, visiting Europe on a study-tour in 1872, put the point more directly:

We come to study your strength, that, by adopting widely your better ways, we may hereafter be stronger ourselves . . .

Japan has succeeded brilliantly in adopting and adapting Western technology and institutions, but after more than a century of close and continuing contact with the West, the country remains not merely distinct but somehow also separate and apart. Lord Curzon, the British diplomat who was acknowledged in his day as a leading expert on Asian affairs, warned as long ago as 1896 that Japan would not long remain content to be the grateful pupil of the West — "the more she has assimilated European excellence, the more critical she has become of European defects". But criticisms have been muted. The more frequent Japanese response to the West has been one of uncertainty and puzzlement, coupled with a desire not to seem out of step with the rest. Japan's attempt to keep on good terms with all nations, to trade everywhere and offend no one, has led to charges that its foreign policy lacks not only direction but even principles.

Yet Japan is irrevocably committed to the international economy. A nation which imports such massive quantities of oil, food and raw materials cannot be self-sufficient. And a necessary consequence of international economic involvement is a growing, if still very limited, internationalization of Japanese society. By 1981 more than 445,000 Japanese were living overseas, representing an increase of 120,000 over the course of a decade. 40% of them live in South America and 30% in North America. Less than 12% live in Asia, however, and less than 11% in Western Europe, and most of these are temporary residents, whereas a large proportion of those in the Americas are permanent. Whether Japanese who have lived abroad do, in fact, alter the outlook of their countrymen is another question. The longer they have lived away from Japan, the more fluent they are in foreign languages, the less solidly "Japanese" they may seem.

A survey of Japanese attitudes to foreign visi-

Restaurant in Hokkaido. Foreign styles have novelty value.

tors, conducted on behalf of the Prime Minister's Office in 1980, showed that only 4% of the respondents had contact with foreigners at the time of the survey, that 21% said they would like to have contact with foreigners and that 64% said they had no intention of seeking further contact with foreigners. Generally speaking, older and less educated people had less desire to associate with foreigners than did the young and highly educated. When it came to the possible marriage of a close relative to a foreigner, 38% were entirely opposed, 23% were in favour, 10% said it depended on the nationality and 29% were undecided. These figures must be interpreted with caution. A lack of interest in associating with foreigners need not spring from hostility but from a keen fear of possible embarrassment. Opposition to

TV studios — Japan imports many foreign programmes but Japanese productions are rarely seen abroad. Here technicians prepare the set for an episode of a samurai drama series.

mixed marriages can be based on a realistic concern with the difficulties involved in changing long-established social customs.

Visits by foreigners are welcomed by the vast majority of Japanese, but the employment of foreigners in Japan is not viewed with favour, unless you bring some special skill needed by employers. With regard to the naturalization of non-Japanese, most of the respondents to the survey pronounced themselves neutral, and those in favour of such a policy (37%) greatly outnumbered those against. In all the various matters touched on by the survey the most positive and friendly attitudes towards foreigners were held by those who where young and well-educated and had travelled abroad. This may suggest that over the coming years such attitudes may become more general among the population of Japan as a whole.

"Foreigner" is, however, a large category, and not at all the same as "Westerner". Because the great majority of Japanese must learn English at school, because literally tens of thousands of

books written in European languages are translated into Japanese each year, the Japanese have a strong respect for Western culture, even if the political and economic behaviour of Western countries is often difficult to get along with. But Japan's own cultural traditions incorporate strong elements of Buddhism and Confucianism and its largest markets and sources of imports are in East and South East Asia. Relations with the countries of this region are clouded by the memory of war-time conquest and occupation.

But in recent years Japan has been seen in this area as a major source of high technology and development aid, not only by resource-rich countries such as Indonesia but also by much poorer nations, like Burma and Bangladesh.

As an economic super-power accounting for some 10% of the world's output, Japan is constantly being pressed by other developed nations to play a more active role in international affairs. The ways in which the Japanese respond to this pressure will have far-reaching implications for the peoples of both the developed and the developing countries. Japan has long shown itself willing to learn from foreigners. Increasingly, it is being asked to assume the role of teacher. Are foreigners now willing to learn from Japan?

THE JAPANESE ARE COMING

... what she has achieved ... meets with but scant recognition among the manufacturers and merchants of Great Britain, who have failed alike to recognise the already great and always growing importance of Japan as a market for their own products or the possibility of her becoming a formidable competitor with them ....

(D. Murray, 1906)

The Japanese are not coming. The Japanese have arrived. By the early 1980s there were more than 350 Japanese businesses operating in Britain. Most, it is true, were only branches or subsidiaries of major Japanese banks, insurance companies and trading houses, but more than twenty were in manufacturing industry, representing an investment of the order of £1,000 million.

Not surprisingly, electronics and, in particular, the manufacture of colour TV sets, led the field, with factories turning out the products of such well-known firms as Sony, Mitsubishi and National Panasonic. But one of the first to have been established was YKK, the zip manufacturer; and other Japanese-run factories were making goods as varied as spectacle lenses and photo-copiers, cassette tapes and ball-bearings, fire-alarms and fishing-tackle. Some of these factories have been located in "new" industrial areas, like Toshiba's colour TV plant at Plymouth; but many are located in regions whose traditional industries have gone into decline. The largest single concentration of Japanese factories is in Wales. Scotland, the north-west and the Tyne-Tees area are also favoured locations.

Just as Wales has the largest concentration of Japanese factories in Britain, so Britain as a whole has the largest concentration in Europe. The 6,000 or so people employed in Japanese-managed factories in Britain outnumber the total workforce of Japanese factories in the rest of Europe.

But Japan's economic presence is becoming increasingly a European phenomenon. The Nissan motor company, which exports to Europe under the name "Datsun", is involved in truck manufacture in Spain and car production in Italy. Nippon Electric has plants in Ireland and West Germany. Although this trend is likely to continue, Britain will probably retain its favoured position as the key area for Japanese investment and operations, partly because English is the foreign language that Japanese are most familiar with, partly because the country enjoys such excellent communications with Europe and the rest of the world, and partly perhaps because London is still one of the world's leading centres of commercial and financial trading and information. Other reasons may include the special financial inducements given to companies willing to create jobs in areas of high unemployment and the increasingly evident desire of British governments and corporations to co-operate with Japanese firms in such advanced technology fields as telecommunications and robotics and in jointly promoting business in fast-developing regions such as Africa and the Middle East, where Britain has long-established connections and experience. The tie-up between Honda and British Leyland which produced the Triumph "Acclaim" may be only one of many such arrangements in future years.

As Japan's economy has become more and more involved in international trade, so Japanese companies have themselves begun to internationalize both their operations and their workforce. By 1981, of the Minolta camera company's 9,000 employees, for instance, one in five was non-Japanese. TDK, a world-leader in the production of cassette and video-tapes, had overseas factories in Taiwan, Korea, the United States, Mexico and Brazil. Its British subsidiary, however, had only one Japanese member of staff, although four of the British employees were sent each year to Japan for training. The Seiko watch company, based at Guildford, had some 200 employees, of whom only four were Japanese.

Japanese investment in Britain not only creates jobs, it also helps Britain's export trade. Although Japanese TV manufacturers' output of 670,000 sets in 1979 represented only just over a third of the total British market, 150,000 were exported, accounting for five sixths of total British exports of TV sets. About 80% of the zips produced by YKK are also exported. At the NSK ball-bearing factory at Peterlee, Co. Durham the proportion of exports is even higher — 85%. And when the hi-fi maker, Aiwa, opened its Newport works in 1980 it announced that at least half of its output would be intended for Europe.

Japanese companies are also keen to contribute to the communities of which they are a part. NSK has encouraged local horticultural societies to grow prize chrysanthemums, which are the national flower of Japan. Sharp Electronics has sponsored a soccer school in Manchester, where Bobby Charlton and leading FA coaches train local teenagers. Mitsui celebrated the centenary of its London office by donating thousands of Asian elm trees resistant to the Dutch elm disease which had devastated the English countryside in the 1970s.

Japanese manufacturers in Britain have been successful. In seven years TDK managed to capture 30% of the UK market for over-the-counter sales of cassette tapes and saw their turnover grow by 40 times and their gross profit by 80 times. Between 1975 and 1980 Seiko increased its UK sales ten-fold. And, as the Director-General of the Japan External Trade Organisation has pointed out:

> Of all the Japanese manufacturing companies in Britain only one has ever suffered from industrial action, and that was not because of any protest from within the company but because the union was instructed by its national headquarters in connection with problems in other plants, not the Japanese one.

The success of Japanese companies in Britain has confounded sceptics who believed it would be impossible for Japanese executives, with expectations of total worker commitment, to cope with British workers whose outlook has been conditioned by an historic antagonism between labour and management. Japanese managers have, in fact, shown themselves well aware of the need to take account of local conditions and have not tried simply to transplant a Japanese-style operation onto foreign soil. But they have made changes and while some have been accepted only slowly, others have won instant approval. The Japanese passion for uniforms can seem dehumanizing to the individualistic British, but attitudes can change when the wearing of uniforms by workers and managers alike is appreciated as part of a philosophy of eliminating status differences which also requires everyone to "clock on", to eat in the same canteen and to use the same washroom facilities. As the Japanese head of Toshiba's UK operations put it:

> The only kind of 'them and Us' situation we want . . . is one where 'them' is the competition and 'us' is everyone working for Toshiba.

According to the journalist Dick Wilson, the presence of the Japanese is significant because what they "offer us is not so much an import of Japanese methods but rather a stimulus to reform British methods and to free them from inhibiting and clogging factors such as the restrictive aspects of trade unionism and class antagonism". A senior British executive with seven years' experience of working for Japanese companies in Britain has put the same point even more forcefully:

> We can't help looking at the standards set by our parent company in Japan, which makes us ask the question: 'If they can do it, why can't we . . . ?'

STATISTICAL COMPARISONS

POPULATION (1982)	JAPAN	USA	UK
Area ('000 square kilometres)	378	9,363	244
Population (millions)	118.45	232.06	55.78
Population density (persons per sq. km)	313	25	229
Annual rate of increase (%) (1972-80)	1.1	na	0
Persons per average household	3.22	na	2.9
Life expectancy (years)	74.22 (male)	70.5 (male)	70.4 (male)
	79.66 (female)	78.1 (female) (1980)	76.6 (female) (1978-80)

GROSS NATIONAL PRODUCT			
GNP (US $ billion) (1982)	1,060.0	3,059.3	473.8
GNP per head (US $) (1981)	9,684	12,783	9,032
Average annual growth (%) (1977-81)	4.9	3.0	0.4

FOOD INTAKE (grammes per person per day)

	JAPAN (1981)	USA (1978)
Cereals	308	182
Rice	213	—
Potatoes	82	122
Sugar	61	167
Pulses	23	19
Vegetables	309	260
Fruits	167	206
Meat	62	320
Eggs	40	45
Fish and shellfish	96	21
Milk and dairy products	178	718
Fats and oils	40	63
Total calories	2,520	3,393

RESEARCH AND DEVELOPMENT EXPENDITURE (1980)

	JAPAN	USA	UK (1978)
US $ million	20,652	61,127	6,955
As % of national income	2.42	2.61	2.47
%.funded by government	25.8	47.9	48.1

FOREIGN AID TO DEVELOPING COUNTRIES (1980)

	JAPAN	UK
Total (US $ million)	3,304	1,785
As % GNP	0.32	0.34

DEFENCE SPENDING (1980)

	JAPAN	UK
Total (US $ million)	8,960	24,448
Per capita (US $)	75	437
As % government spending	5.2	10.7
As % GNP	0.9	4.9

% JAPANESE HOUSEHOLDS OWNING:	1970	1983
Refrigerators	89.1	99.0
Washing machines	91.4	98.2
TV sets:		
Colour	26.3	98.8
Black and white	90.2	22.8 (1980)
Vacuum cleaners	68.3	95.8
Electric fans	83.2	95.4 (1980)
Cameras	64.1	85.0
Tape recorders	30.8	61.9 (1980)
Cars	22.1	62.9
Stereos	31.2	59.0
Air conditioners	5.9	49.6
Microwave ovens	2.1	37.2
Pianos	6.8	17.4

DISTRIBUTION OF INCOMES (1980)

Households with annual incomes of	%
Less than ¥1,000,000	6.9
¥1,000,000 to ¥2,000,000	15.5
¥2,000,000 to ¥3,000,000	21.9
¥3,000,000 to ¥4,000,000	19.9
¥4,000,000 to ¥5,000,000	14.2
¥5,000,000 to ¥6,000,000	8.9
¥6,000,000 to ¥7,000,000	4.6
Over ¥7,000,000	8.1

NB This table takes no account of the number of persons per household.

Map of Modern Prefectures

1. Hokkaido
2. Tōhoku
3. Kantō
4. Hokuriku
5. Tōsan
6. Tokai
7. Kinki
8. Chūgoku
9. Shikoku
10. Kyūshū
11. Okinawa

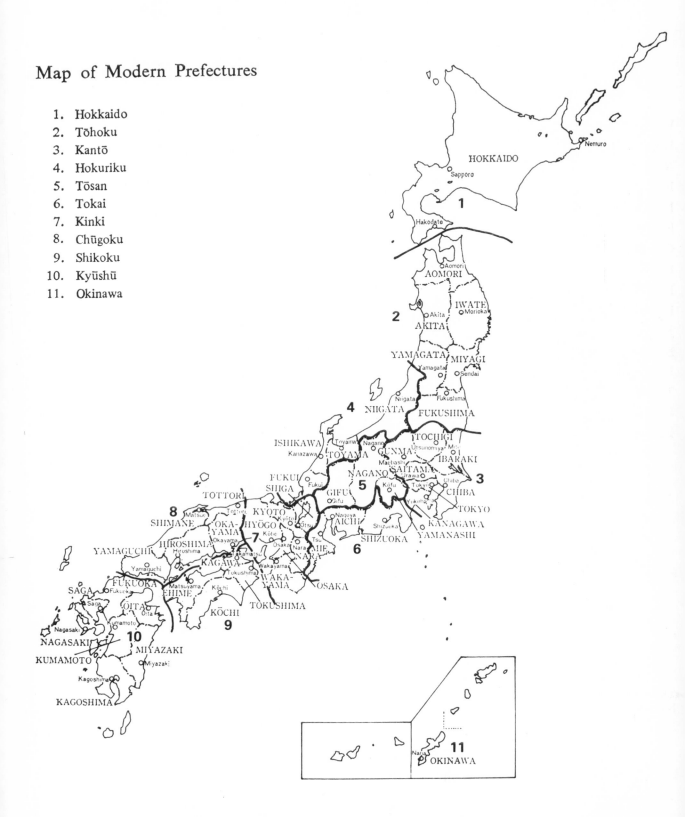

BOOKS FOR FURTHER READING

W.G. Beasley, *The Modern History of Japan* (Weidenfeld & Nicolson)

H.Befu, *Japan: An Anthropological Introduction* (Chandler Publishing Company)

R.P. Dore, *British Factory — Japanese Factory* (Allen & Unwin)

R.P. Dore, *Shinohata: a portrait of a Japanese village* (Allen Lane)

F. Gibney, *Japan: the fragile superpower* (Norton)

N.Ike, *Japan: The New Superstate* (W.H. Freeman)

C. Nakane, *Japanese Society* (Penguin)

E.O. Reischauer, *The Japanese* (Harvard University Press)

K. Shiba, *Oh, Japan!* (Paul Norbury Publications)

Howard Smith (ed), *Inside Japan* (BBC)

J.A.A. Stockwin, *Japan: divided politics in a growth economy* (Weidenfeld & Nicolson)

Richard Tames, *Japan in the Twentieth Century* (Batsford)

Richard Tames, *The Japan Handbook: A Guide for Teachers* (Paul Norbury Publications)

T. Tsurutani, *Political Change in Japan* (Longman)

Ezra F. Vogel, *Japan as No 1: Lessons for America* (Harvard University Press)

Endymion Wilkinson, *Misunderstanding: Europe vs Japan* (Chuokoron-Sha)

◄The map shows prefectures by name and regions by number.

INDEX